CANCER IN TWO VOICES

What Critics Have Already Said . . .

"This landmark feminist perspective on breast cancer . . . is an indictment of the medical profession's casual attitude to women's illness, and also a touching chronicle of two women in their forties grappling intellectually and emotionally with premature death."   —*Publishers Weekly*

"The book is impressive in its detailed account of the way two women involved their community in their battle, for their sake and for that of their friends. . . . The honesty of the work, along with their courage to explore every pain and emotion, transcends self-importance and pulls the reader into their circle of intimates."   —*San Francisco Chronicle*

"This collection of journal entries, letters, and essays records the intensely personal, painful, and powerful journey Butler and Rosenblum took when Rosenblum was diagnosed with breast cancer. . . . Highly recommended for all public libraries and special collections on women and on death and dying."   —*Library Journal*

"*Cancer in Two Voices* is essential reading for anyone dealing with death and dying, or for anyone simply seeking to find a way to 'enjoy the tenderness and the preciousness of every moment.' Barbara Rosenblum died on February 14, 1988 . . . but her gift of life and love—her voice—lives on."
                    —*Seattle Gay News*

". . . a powerful, compassionate call to living fully in the moment and engaging with all the choices life offers—a book with tremendous healing potential."   —*A Different Light Review*

"*Cancer in Two Voices* . . . is a heartbreaking account of Rosenblum's courageous fight with cancer and Butler's attempts to come to terms with the
situation. Told in the form of essays, journal entries and letters, it is a work
of pain, compassion, courage, even some laughter."

— The Canadian Jewish News

"*Cancer in Two Voices* is not an easy book to read. Nor is it a neat book, just
as living and dying with cancer is not a neat and tidy experience. . . .
Although filled with grief and loss, *Cancer in Two Voices* does not evoke
desperation. Rather, our hearts open to embrace the pain, sadness and
goodness of Barbara and Sandy, as we vow to strengthen our own
commitment to living life in the fullest."   *— New Directions for Women*

"As much about friendship and community as about the experience of
cancer, the book is powerfully, beautifully, and painfully constructed. To
read it is to encounter reactions to widely varied experiences: anger at the
health-care system, gratitude for supportive friends and communities,
sadness at seeing such a rich, intensely felt life cut short. . . . The spirit and
passion of this deeply felt and imaginative work, a lasting honor to
Rosenblum's memory, can instruct and challenge many—cancer patients,
families, and caregivers alike."   *— Medical Humanities Review*

"In a narrow sense, one could say that *Cancer in Two Voices* is specifically
about a lesbian couple living with breast cancer. However, the range of
issues confronted, the quality of writing, and the effectiveness of their
strategies, make this book relevant to a much broader audience. It could be
useful reading for both practitioners and scholars concerned with life-
threatening, debilitating, or chronic illnesses. It can also serve as a valuable
resource for patients, families, and friends confronted with such illnesses.
Already popular with lesbian and feminist audiences, it deserves a wide
range of readership."   *— Disability Studies Quarterly*

"And although cancer is ever present, this book is about so much more than
coping with a disease. . . . It is about family, about choices, about disorder,
conflict and uncertainty; a book about the struggle to love and live in the
face of great tragedy or simply the complexities of our everyday lives. A
remarkable achievement, *Cancer in Two Voices* extends a kind of lifeline
not only to those of us touched immediately by cancer or other life-
threatening illness, but to anyone struggling to make a meaningful life."

— Bridges

"It's a sad book, true, but it's also loving, enabling, and inspiring. . . . The
book is a little miracle, too, and should be read by every woman still lucky
enough to be alive."   *— Women's Library Workers Journal*

"*Cancer in Two Voices* is lucid, pedantic, and enormously powerful   In the last section, Butler's palpable grief deserves more space. Finally, there is no fictive pretense between writer and reader; the authors have taken on the risk of self-exposure with complete eloquence. Their truths become our truths."   —*Lambda Book Report*

"This is a proud book. A book about loving and living. The failures recorded here are not failures of love or imagination or strength; they are failures in the systems we have been taught to trust, most conspicuously, Western medicine . . ."   —*Sojourner*

"This unusual, gripping, and beautifully written book is a valuable document for cancer patients, their families, friends, social workers, and other health care providers . . . It is also a tribute to Dr. Rosenblum's courage and perseverance and to the love and devotion of her life partner, Sandra Butler, the author of *Conspiracy of Silence*, one of the first books to expose the prevalence of incest. . . . I strongly recommend this book for its riveting insight into the heart and mind of two very thoughtful, sensitive women who dealt with tragedy with love, humor, courage, anger, pain and finally, resignation to the force of death to which we must all eventually succumb."
—*Clinical Social Work Journal*

"The book is an intense chronicle of joy, hope, grief, loss, desperation, despair, resolution, and rage. Nothing is edited or spared. No feelings are too inappropriate to print; no secrets are held back. As a seasoned hospice nurse, I thought I was accustomed to pain, but this book broke my heart. The authors are lesbians—a long-invisible group in health care—but their feelings of fear and anguish are universal. . . . Readers of all sexual orientations will identify and weep with these authors."   —*Hospice Magazine*

"It's an extraordinarily moving and profound book for anyone interested in the examined life. . . . Painful though their story is, it's not depressing, but rather inspiring because of each woman's extraordinary ability to express eloquently feelings of the sort that often 'lie too deep for words.'"
—*Philadelphia Welcomat*

"This may be the most important book that you will read in your life, both for what it tells of Barbara and Sandy's personal experiences, and for what it demands that we do with our own lives. . . . *Cancer in Two Voices* is as much about living fully as it is about dying. . . . To read this book is to embrace life."   —*Bay Area Reporter*

CANCER IN TWO VOICES

SANDRA BUTLER

AND

BARBARA ROSENBLUM

SPINSTERS INK

DULUTH

Second edition.

10-9-8-7-6-5-4-3-2

Spinsters Ink
32 E. First St., #330
Duluth, MN 55802-2002

Portions of this book were previously published, and appear here in slightly different form by kind permission of the publishers. All efforts have been made to cite the correct bibliographic data. Apologies are made for any errors.

Excerpts previously appeared in *New Statesmen*, February 1988, Vol. 115, Issue 2968; *Outlook*, Spring 1988; *Outlook*, Winter 1989; *Sinister Wisdom*, Issue 32, 1987; *Sinister Wisdom*, Issue 33, 1987; *Sinister Wisdom*, Issue 43/44, 1991; *Utne Reader*, September,1991.

"Coming Home" previously appeared as "Reverberations," in *The Tribe of Dina: A Jewish Women's Anthology*, ed. Melanie Kaye/Kantrowitz, Beacon Press, 1989 (used by permission); and in *Out the Other Side: Contemporary Lesbian Writing*, ed. Christian McEwen and Sue O'Sullivan, Crossing Press, 1989.

"Living in an Unstable Body" appears as "Living in a Changing Body" in *An Intimate Wilderness: Lesbian Writers on Sexuality*, ed. Judith Barrington, Eighth Mountain Press, 1991.

Cover Photo by Deborah Hunter

Production for Second Edition:	Claire Kirch	Marian Hunstiger
	Helen Dooley	Erika Thorne
	Joan Drury	Liz Tufte
		Nancy Walker

Production for First Edition:	Pamela Ai Lin To	Margaret Livingston
	Jennifer Bennett	Joan Meyers
	Theresa Gradine	Linda Moschell
	Laura Green	Camille Pronger
	Jeannette Howard	Sherry Thomas

Library of Congress Cataloging In Publication Data

Butler, Sandra,1938–
Cancer in two voices / Sandra Butler and Barbara Rosenblum.—[2nd ed.]
    p.   cm.
ISBN 1-883523-16-8 (alk. paper)
1. Rosenblum, Barbara, 1943-1988—Health. 2. Breast—Cancer—Patients—United States—
Biography. 3. Butler, Sandra, 1938– 4. Lesbian couples—United States.
I. Rosenblum, Barbara, 1943-1988.   II. Title.
RC280.B8B85   1996
362.1'9699449'0092—dc20
[B]   96-36588
                                                                                           CIP

CANCER IN TWO VOICES

ACKNOWLEDGMENTS

My life with Barbara was embedded in friendship, in connectedness, in community. Those we loved were the cushion upon which we rested and strengthened ourselves. There are hundreds of such women and men, and I am deeply grateful for their presence in my life. There are several I want to mention by name:

Ruth Rosenblum, Stan Deneroff, Marcia Freedman, Gail Hornstein, Jane Ariel, Berenice Fisher, and Joyce Lindenbaum, who read and re-read with patience and insistence that these words be shaped with skill and honed with truth. They kept both of us honest before, during, and after.

Deena Metzger, the first to describe parts of this journey and who gently insisted I stay close to the bone.

Jackie Winnow, whose passion, sense of outrage, and political acumen has been a beacon for me.

Myra Wise and Donald Cliggett, who held our hands and walked us through.

Janaea and Alison, my daughters, blessing and miracle.

Asher, who has the gift of Barbara's legacy and love.

Congregation Sha'ar Zahav, an in-gathering whose time has finally come.

Cottages at Hedgebrook, which allowed me space, time, beauty, and silence so that Barbara's presence might return to prod, remind, urge, whisper, laugh, and edit as I completed our book.

Annie Hershey and Lucy Massie Phenix, who crafted the video Barbara and I made three weeks before her death and continue to remind me of the healing properties of the creative impulse.

This book was completed with the support and encouragement of The Wandering Menstruals, my consciousness-raising group, who give a radical, thoughtful, and joyous shape to my fifth decade.

There were those who formed Barbara's and my support group, fed us, took us on walks, listened patiently, gave us parties, and dressed up in silk to go dancing. I cherish you all. Jeanne Adleman, Sandy Boucher, Lauren and Mark Chaitkin, Marinell Eva, Ingrid Foeken, Nan Fink, M.J. Hanafin, Judy Herman, Melanie Kaye/ Kantrowitz, Helen Longino, Linda Marks, Valerie Miner, David Pittman, Pam Miller, Susan Rennie, Diana Russell, Rachelle Ruthschild, Arlene Shmaeff, Judy Stein, Riek Stienstra, Rosalie Walls, Linda Wilson, and Mark Zeitschik.

Sherry Thomas, for her dedication to the world of feminist publishing, her critical intelligence, and patience in the process. Joan Meyers, for her meticulous and loving attention to every detail. And Sembei, our dog. Thank you.

For Barbara:
zichrona l'bracha
Blessed is her memory.

Contents

INTRODUCTION

On Valentine's Day, February 14, 1988, Barbara Rosenblum died. She was my partner, my friend, my love. Now I sit at a computer trying to carve shape and substance into the cold marble of memory. I sift through scraps of paper, journal entries, recorded dreams, photographs, medical records, tapping and clicking in patterns that I hope will allow you to enter the world we inhabited together, to see parts of yourselves in us, and perhaps to love more fully and deeply because of all we learned.

In February of 1985, when Barbara told our friends of her diagnosis of advanced breast cancer, she said that statistically she was only the first. "Many of my friends will see their future in the way I handle mine. There will be others. It is only a matter of time."

It was then that we chose to write this book as a map of our experiences in the hopes that it would be of use to those of you now reading it. We wanted to tell you our story. Or at least some of our story. A story about struggle and courage, even more than the part about sickness and death. A story about loss and the gifts it brings. We wanted to tell our story, finally, because this writing made us visible to ourselves as we were living it.

But this is also the history of our loving: of dancing together to rock and roll, of making bouillabaisse and growing tomatoes in the garden, of finding unexpected messages under pillows, dishes, in coat pockets. This is a story of two ordinary women who found love in each other, then in themselves. And who began to heal.

As the surviving partner, the inevitable task of accompanying you, the reader, through this journey, falls to me. My hope is that my words will illuminate our experience, bridge some moments, clarify others.

Barbara and I started to write within days after her diagnosis of advanced breast cancer—understanding that "attention must be paid" to this, as yet, unrecorded experience. There was little discussion about beginning to write. We simply began.

The book begins with the first writing Barbara and I did together, two years before her diagnosis. It is a meditation on Jewish identity, the meanings of home, and the life we created together. Then sections alternate between our journal entries and longer sustained reflections about the life that was racing past us. These reflections were an attempt to fix meaning, to slow down the process, to enrich our understanding.

Barbara and I met in 1979, at a time when her life was in fragments and filled with uncertainty. She was then an assistant professor at Stanford who had just been denied tenure and was ending a significant relationship. I had just moved from San Francisco to Palo Alto when my youngest daughter graduated from high school and left to live in Israel. This odd confluence of beginnings and endings was not an immediate connection, however. We were both wary, distrustful, uncertain—having learned too many sad lessons in loving.

But there was much to connect us—odd juxtapositions that caused the tension of our ambivalence to soften. We were both Jews—she from a progressive, first-generation immigrant family, and I from a middle-class, assimilated, suburban one. Neither of us, we discovered, had been in a temple for over a decade.

Both of us were urban women, having lived in New York, Chicago, San Francisco, and Boston in the past two decades. Both of us had lived as heterosexuals, with increasing numbers of love affairs with women during the ten years prior to our meeting.

She was sharp, mordant, witty, and playful at the book publication party at which we met. She was also eccentrically dressed and wore one sock inside out. Her energy was electrifying, her intellect compelling. We talked, I remember, about Judy Chicago, an artist whose show had recently opened in San Francisco, about fine food, feminism, violence against women, *klezmer* music, social class—hers and mine. We began on that day to talk. Over the next month, during the coffee dates, the walks, the movies, our words formed an avalanche. And so it remained for the next nine years.

Barbara and I were our own parenthesis—cradling the "us" within it. She was contemplative, cerebral. I, extravagant, public. We balanced, heightened, buttressed, challenged those dimensions in each other with tenderness, impatience, anger, and much humor.

During the first years we were together, our words crashed around us, often leaving us feeling uncertain about what we were doing together. We were such an unlikely couple. But finally, the words began to cut away at the underbrush of her anxiety and my depression. Her reticence and my bravado. Her determined bohemianism and my equally dogged political righteousness. As layer upon layer eroded and wound upon wound was revealed, we arrived at those most precious moments—visible to each other. This was a visibility we had hungered for all our lives. The loneliness that had been our oldest companion lifted and the partnershhip—the "us"—replaced it.

We remained an odd couple, unlikely, perhaps, to those who did not know us well. We retained our separate friends, our own priorities, our own political emphases. That is what made the "us" work so well. Like a bellows, we awoke each morning to embrace, our first conscious act a movement towards the other. Then we rose to begin days that expanded to include other people, ideas, travel, writing, teaching, activism. At night, we again bent towards each other over the dinner table, carefully chosen words translating our experiences. Even after Barbara became ill, and we began to travel together, the pattern we had established remained constant. She found the botanical gardens and the museums and I sought out the women's bookstores and cafes. Then at dinner, the cascade of words brought "us" in.

There was much air and space and movement in our "us." For six years, before Barbara's diagnosis, we fought and cried, loved and played—all to the counterpoint of words. Angry words, frightened words, intimate code words, analytic words, loving words. They were our currency, our medium. This book is filled with the words of the "us" that began with Barbara's diagnosis and ended with her death.

One year after Barbara's death, I returned to the carefully stacked journals, piles of letters bound with rubber bands, letters we had written to each other and to friends, file drawers filled with unfinished essays, and began to prepare our words for publication. I was uncertain about how to ease the awkward transitions—the pauses in narrative. This experience was not smooth. Or graceful. Nor was Barbara. It was uneven, unexpected. Choppy, filled with wide emotional swings. That is more the truth than fluid and sustained journal entries. Consequently, there has been only a little weeding, pruning, removal of excess. It's all here. As we lived it together. Untidy. As two lives are. These words are our legacy offered to you, with love.

Now I understand that Barbara was right. It was only a matter of time, and she was only the first. There have been many others—in our life together and now in mine. Every fifteen minutes in the United States, a woman dies of breast cancer; one out of every nine women will be diagnosed in her lifetime. This year alone [1990] 44,500 women will die of breast cancer. This is already a shared epidemic—a collective experience.

But, finally, this isn't just a book about cancer, and it isn't really a book about dying either. It's a book about living expansively, openheartedly, joyfully in the face of our inevitable death. Instead of looking for miracles, we can each become our own miracle.

Foreword: Letter to Barbara

April 9, 1996 –
WHAT SHOULD HAVE BEEN YOUR 53RD BIRTHDAY

Dear Barbara,

You planted purple iris to welcome me when I moved into your apartment seventeen years ago. Your back yard was a chaotic 10' x 15' vegetable garden, hospitable home to arugula, tomatoes, mint, radishes, all in no particular order. And always, in the midst of the clutter, from the very beginning, was a large green plastic trash bag. I came to rely on its presence as the symbol of a miniature world, always in movement, never finished—even for the day. Every few years, you designed a new garden, interspersing fruits and vegetables, flowers and spices, all aligned perfectly on the yellow-lined paper. We drove to a nursery for the supplies necessary to translate this elegant drawing into our small stretch of dirt. And the project lasted until your book review, article, teaching schedule, or trip took you, with equal excitement, into the next activity, the overflowing green plastic garbage bag, tilted in the center of the garden, awaiting your enthusiastic return.

My life has been in movement too, Barbara. Three years ago I left our home. As each room yielded up the vulnerable stain of darkened paint under the pictures propped against the walls, they turned into cobwebby, dusty receptacles—preparing to be painted and papered for the next set of lives, the next set of voices that will fill them. The garden was also in movement when I left, Barbara. Weeds were pushing their way through the dirt as they always successfully insist upon doing. Your ashes were blended with the soil that had brought forth the iris, the cherry tomato, the flowering daphne. The garden was in waiting for the next family to turn its soil, to plant the seeds deep within it, to nourish it. Life will return to that yard, and you will be a part of it.

In 1991, when *Cancer in Two Voices* was first published, I traveled across the country to women's bookstores, college campuses, and health centers to speak about our life and your death. About the public nature of private disease. To insist upon honoring the unique dimensions of lesbian experience and to create respectful and relevant legal and medical resources for us and for our families. To bring women into our particular world while embedding that world in the largest understanding of life and of death. To remind the reader that we all breathe the same air, eat the same mass-produced foods, drink the same water. That we all inhabit the same planet, and our shared task is to make the world safe and habitable. Every room I entered was filled to overflowing with women eager to tell me, and more important, one another, about the deaths that shaped their lives. Women eager to develop a vocabulary both psychological and existential, a vocabulary that would help them negotiate the inevitability of personal loss as well as the outrage necessary to mobilize against the reality of so much unnecessary death.

Now there is an avalanche of women with breast cancer. Scarcely a week passes that another diagnosis is not wailed into the phone, murmured at a party. A letter arrives, explaining a month-long silence. Some of these women have small and contained cancers requiring lumpectomy and radiation, others have already metastasized tumors, demanding that yet another woman in the midst of her life, prepare for its end. The form, the womanly shape of a circle that surrounded us in your dying, has become terrifyingly commonplace now. As have the services, organizations, conferences, books, articles, videotapes. Cancer is now a deadly fact in the lives of middle-aged women. No one is untouched, Barbara. Cancer does not startle now.

Our book opened a floodgate in women who had not yet seen their lives on the page. Our pages allowed that mirror, Barbara. Everything we had hoped our jottings, diary entries, private musings would release, has happened. Yesterday, I went into my local bookstore and saw, just inside the front door, a prominent display of books about breast cancer. Political books, the kind you would have wanted to read. Books that didn't exist for us in 1985. Our video has been shown in gay and lesbian as well as Jewish film festivals all over the world. So many people have been touched and moved by reading our words. I know, because they tell me everywhere I go.

The task of making the private experience of cancer public, and therefore political, has been engaged, Barbara. Women with breast cancer no longer yield to the inevitability of living in an environment that is filled with carcinogenic food, air, water. Lesbians living with breast cancer are no longer willing to be limited to individual solutions based on organic fruits and vegetables, exercise, and a balanced regimen of work and play, meditative rest, and carefully calibrated activity. Our lives, your death, and this book have been a pivotal part in developing the consciousness necessary to engage the terrible urgency of political activism. At a recent demonstration of breast cancer activists, the streets were filled with women whose lives had been altered by a diagnosis of breast cancer. There were husbands, parents, children, friends, and lesbian partners expanding the idea of family. There were physicians and nurses marching alongside health consumers affirming patients' rights to respectful, collaborative treatment. Placards and chants insisted on health care for everyone, that insurance cover preventive mammograms, that there be increased funding for research, for the development of alternative treatments, and the construction of safety nets for poor women, lesbians, women who speak little or no English and cannot find their illness, their lives in the texts or the resources. They were all in the street, Barbara, and they were impolite, insistent, and their numbers are growing.

Everything is in movement. Like the green plastic garbage bag poised to receive what is no longer necessary for the garden's flowering, leaving room for new growth. As I left our home, my last act was to place your lit yartzeit candle gently in the corner of the garden. I said a final prayer as the flame flickered in the slight wind that moved through the small yard. I thanked you for all that you, in your living and dying, allowed me. There is a movement now, Barbara. A political, activist movement. You were right. You were the first, and we watched you carefully to see how to live our dying years with elegance, with whimsy, and with a deepened capacity for insisting on what was essential. You taught us, those who watched you, who cared for you, who loved you, all of that and more. Your capacity for exuberant pleasure never flagged, even in the face of your imminent death. Your capacity for joy, for glee, for ticklish fun. I learned that, too. I still remember how, two weeks before you died, you entertained me by transforming your exhausted body into Martha and every single one of the Vandellas. As I climbed up the rickety wooden backstairs for the last time and drove across the Bay Bridge to my new home, my new life, my future, I blessed you, Barbara.

I concluded the Introduction to this book by suggesting that rather than looking for miracles, we each become our own miracle. I continue to learn that my attempts to remain open to all the movement of life is what allows the miraculous to enter. I can tolerate, even sometimes allow, uncertainty and impotence, frustration and despair. I am increasingly successful in staying in the present tense. Your dying taught me much about miracles and about loving in the present tense, and it has served me well in these years of epidemic and loss.

Soon I will be 60, Barbara. I hold the image of that trash bag, rakishly tilted, waiting to be filled. I remember that messy, joyful, constantly evolving garden in movement through the life and death cycle. Of life in process. Increasingly, I can hold it all.

With my love,

Sandy

Coming Home: 1983

Sandy

We both thought that our joining would represent "coming home": a place to rest where we didn't have to explain everything, where we would be understood, where our samenesses would balance (somehow) our differences. But instead we found that our homes were furnished differently. I found myself living in overheated and overstuffed rooms filled with silent others and unfinished dreams. The mirrors that were to reflect us in each other are cloudy and scratched, and we cannot always see where we are going or remember where we have been.

Barbara

I know she will say it's like a mirror, like looking at yourself in a mirror. It's not that way for me. It's more like two diamonds, each of which is spinning around. Maybe like a *dreydl* or dice, and I don't know which side will be up when it stops moving. Sometimes, only sometimes, does my Jewish or lesbian side match her Jewish or lesbian side. More often, it is a mismatch: my lower-class facet faces her maternal side, or my spare, tight, conceptual, academic side faces her dramatic, flamboyant, emotional side. The same rubbing against, the same reaching out and not connecting, the same as in all other relationships. Is it like coming home? Only sometimes.

But when it is, it is powerful, rich, sustaining, fulfilling. It is a connection of a sort unlike any other. A *mechaye!*

When I was fifteen, I was already reading Mark Twain and Thomas Wolfe. They imprinted in me the stories of American injustice, the inherent wrongness of slavery, and a passionate sense of the possibilities of human freedom. I had already learned that being a Jew meant seeing these injustices and doing something about them.

My parents first sent me to Hebrew school but I rebelled at once. A year later, I was sent to Jewish cultural school, *shule.* The teacher was a progressive Jewish man, a survivor, making a living in America by teaching. How I hated it! The room was dark and smelled wet. Not enough electric lighting, one or two bare bulbs in the ceiling. We had to learn Jewish culture and some Yiddish songs. I could not bear the smell. Each day as I passed those girls I wanted to be my friends, laughing together in the school playground watching the boys play football, I was dressed like a poor immigrant kid in hand-me-downs. We were still very poor then. I wore funny-colored leggings and other girls pointed and laughed at me. That was to shape my sense of myself as an outsider. As marginal. A sense of myself that remains still central.

Sandy

It was different in my house. We were scrubbing to erase all traces of the *shtetl.* An elaborate training to leave behind and yet still be with "my own kind." A search that has taken nearly half my lifetime. Admonitions still ring in my ears, hissed nervously for fear/of fear.

"Don't holler out the window."

"Don't draw attention to yourself in a public place."

"Don't talk with your hands." (The irony now is that one of my daughters is a dancer and talks with her entire body.) But always it was a struggle to keep balance. Being Jewish but not "too Jewish." Everyone in my suburb was Jewish, of course. We were to go to school together, to temple together, to marry together. But it was all to be muted. Well-behaved. Not to be like those "others." Gangsters, entertainers, shysters, communists, troublemakers. Not our sort.

There was always emphasis on good manners and an admonition about passion of all sorts. Intellectual passion was unseemly for a girl since it might frighten off the smart boys.

"It is hard enough to get a boyfriend without being too smart." Words my mother's mother had told her a generation before. The legacy handed down as truth from mother to daughter and again to daughter. Instead, the skills that were valued were those of "drawing the other out." Listening, nodding, smiling, feigning interest in others. Not the impassioned and heated arguments about Poland, Stalin, Israel, and the Bolsheviks that Barbara remembers. Never.

The rules were lengthy but consistent. Never to interrupt. Never to talk too loudly. Never to be too strident. Never to have a different opinion unless it was couched carefully in a warm, smiling voice. Not to be Jewish (in the bad way). I did understand that there was something dangerous about being Jewish, but during the first dozen years of my life, except for muted conversations about the "camps," which abruptly ended when I entered the room, I didn't know what that danger was.

Barbara

When I read *The Painted Bird*, I was not shocked. I was not even surprised. Those horrendous grotesque stories straight out of the ignorance of the Middle Ages were familiar to me. Did I not grow up hearing about the dumb Polish villagers? My mother laughingly told me how she would ridicule their believing in the sanctified birth of Jesus Christ. "A bastid. They believe in a bastid," she would laugh. Her own syphilitic brother, in the state of paresis and fully delusional, used to roam the streets of the village, talking to ghosts. The villagers laughed at him, the town fool and idiot; they taunted her, "There she goes, the sister of the idiot." When he became unmanageable, my mother remembers, the family locked him in the closet where he withered, shriveled, and soon died.

Is this a story from the twentieth century? I remember now another story. When my mother was a girl in her village and someone got sick, you went to a witch, what we would probably now call an herbalist, perhaps a midwife or a barber. They would burn your back with *bankes* (hot cups), collect odd things, and make potions. When I was a young girl and got sick, my back was badly burned with *bankes*. These were my growing-up stories.

Sandy

When I was thirteen, I had a jukebox in our fully decorated "game room." I used to listen to the music of Nat "King" Cole and sway with my "boyfriend," a broom, preparing myself for the popularity and social success I hoped was awaiting me.

Barbara

While she was thirteen and dancing to popular American music, I was eight and still listening to the Yiddish radio. But I made it. Upward mobility was my way out. My parents wanted the job security of the Civil Service for me, a postal clerk I should become. But I went up through the City College system in New York, that free university that permitted thousands of first- and second-generation Jews to become professionals. I did it too.

Often the difference between Sandy and me is expressed through food. I order fancy wines, exotic cuisines. It's a way of marking how far I have come. We ate poor. Jewish people's poor food: chicken feet stew, beef, lung and heart soup. And *pitcha*: calf's foot jelly smeared on rye bread with a piece of garlic and *shmaltz* was often supper. Beef *flanken* soup packed with bones. When Sandy is out of town on business, I buy a bag of bones in the supermarket and make soup. I call my mother and tell her I made soup. She seems pleased. I still remember the first time I had steak. I was eleven years old. It was a sign we were beginning to become more American. Beginning to assimilate. Steak.

Sandy

We did not eat with our fingers. We did not talk with our mouths full. We did not have "seconds" until all our "firsts" were eaten. We ate roast beef, steak, lamb chops, and mashed potatoes. Every Sunday we went to the Abner Wheeler House for dinner after my mother finished listening to Milton Cross and the opera. I always ordered roast beef and popovers. My brother had steak and mashed potatoes My mother had breast of chicken, very well done and with the skin removed, please. My father drank and nibbled at whatever was put before him. WASP food. A WASP restaurant.

One Sunday my brother loudly showed us the woman at the adjoining table who had a noticeable mustache. Horrified, my mother muttered that now the entire restaurant was staring at us. We were drawing attention to ourselves.

Now, forty years later, I know that we were the only Jews in the restaurant all those Sundays. We sat and were careful not to spill, not to talk too loudly, not to make "them" stare at us. The outsiders. The unwelcome ones. I still don't know why we always went.

Entering Barbara's parents' apartment, I see the walls filled with pictures of the *shtetl*, memories of the loss of a way of life. A home with history in it. Books about the Holocaust. Stories still to be repeated. To be remembered. For me, the Holocaust was an intellectual and emotional immersion into a period of my history that served as a guide for me in formulating my moral, ethical, and political posture in the world. A way to understand what it is, what it means to be a Jew. What the nature of evil is. What the imminent dangers are. What my relationship to the state of Israel, that "sorry miracle," has become. It was an immersion that was both connection and warning. Work that led me directly to engage in the political issues of my own decades. School busing. Civil rights. Vietnam. A sense of the urgency of a principled life. It was a period of heightening the sense of myself as "other." As outsider. As hated Jew. (Not yet woman.) And understanding that even if the *goyim* saw me as a troublemaker, a Zionist scourge, a dirty, aggressive, shrill kike . . . I began to see myself in community with other Jews and a sense of pride emerged. Those of us actively involved in political work during the '60s were the bearers of the torch of freedom and righteousness with other oppressed people. I was an oppressed person. This was a huge leap for the well-behaved, well-modulated, young girl. My immersion in the Holocaust was the beginning of my bonding with all Jews.

Barbara

I know there are many ways to understand the Holocaust, but they all come down to one of two ways: from the outside and from

5

the inside. How come an American Jew like me looks at it (and feels justified to look at it) from the inside? It wasn't until I was in my thirties that I could look at it from the outside, in terms of scholarship, of genocide, or the origins of totalitarianism. Most of my life, I saw it from the inside, from my family, hearing the stories of those who had survived. In the early '50s, my mother spent almost all her time in the courthouse, signing sworn statements about the character of her relatives who were coming to America. One by one, I met them. Emaciated bodies, toothless mouths, metal teeth. I met each one as they came through our house. I went to the beach with them and saw their scarred bodies, Hitler's experiments. One uncle had no ribs on one side of his body. It was an experiment so the German doctors could see how someone might live without ribs. Another woman had no insides. They excavated the flesh of my living relatives. They wrote numbers on their arms. I met each one and learned their stories. Who among them did not almost die? And see their families die?

Each morning before leaving for school, I heard the announcements on the Yiddish radio. A man, Moishe Schwartz from the town of Czecknova, has just arrived. Does anyone remember him? Does anyone know someone from his village? Does he have any living relatives? If you know, please call the radio station. Can anyone please locate a *lantsman* for Mr. Schwartz? Tombstones of the living on the air waves.

For me, I suppose, there has always been the loss. My mother thinks she is lucky because she lives in an apartment with indoor hot and cold running water. She never feels safe and has a recurring dream that she will have no place to sleep at night; she awakens with the same terrified feeling she had as a girl. So there is nothing more to lose. Just to continue to regain. Recapture. Build. And always understand we live on the margin. Always.

Sandy and I walk the streets of San Francisco together and see so many of the same things. While we each come to this moment with so many differences, we see so much of the same thing. Hardships etched into a face. A child looking frightened. A mother trembling with frustration. A window advertising Irish sweaters decorated with sacks of rotten potatoes. Bag ladies. Those who are alone. Marginal, lost, anxious, angry. We turn to each other and silently acknowledge that, "Yes, I see. Yes. We are them too. Yes." It is a very big consolation in a very disorderly world.

Sandy

We have become mother, lover, friend, confidante, partners, playmates. It is too much. And yet, beyond each other is the danger. We use each other to represent "our own kind." There is always the sense of thin ice upon which we walk as confidently as we can, holding tightly to each other's hand.

We ease the passage for each other now. I steer her through the labyrinth of social rules I have memorized since girlhood. She is patient with me in my intellectual hungers. We open doors for each other and allow our arms to circle the other's waist. Just for a moment. I am here with you. Don't worry. I'm on your side. It isn't finally coming home, but making the home we always hungered for.

Only the First

February — April 1985

Sandy
February 19

I am on my way to Winnipeg for a conference. We had, as always, much difficulty separating. Her need of me. Mine of distance. The ways we tear at each other for comfort and reassurance. My fear of losing myself in her need of me.

I have misgivings about all the business travel I have planned for this year. There is a frenzied rush to much of my work that leaves little room for pleasure. I remain harried and unsatisfied, with one task merely leading to the next. For now, I immerse myself in details—lists—notes—but find the usual soothing that results from the accomplishment of assigned tasks elusive.

I'm worried about the changes in Barbara's body but trust—mostly trust—that it is nothing to be alarmed about and that her anxiety is more habitual than necessary. She goes for the results of the second test and needle biopsy tomorrow with Anna, and I'll call after work for the results. No need to worry about it in advance. There will be plenty of time to worry if that becomes necessary.

Barbara

February 20

I am a sociologist and that is a big part of my identity. I was drawn to my discipline because of many natural and instinctive ways I look at the world. I look at systems and their sub-parts and how they all interact. And, mainly, I look at people and figure out what makes them tick.

During my years of formal training to become a sociologist, I learned and developed very fine observational skills. A tone in the voice; the raising of an eyebrow for emphasis; the gesture that accompanies the sentence and gives it meaning and emotion; and something I borrowed from art and philosophy, an appreciation of a person's posture and all its concomitant meanings—that is, the history of the person contained in the posture, the gesture.

I'm very good at my work. And I'm proud of how good I am at reading micro behavior. So when the doctor came into the room, folder in hand, comporting herself firmly and with an air of ordinary, matter-of-fact efficiency, I searched for every clue—every curve in the face, the lines of the eyes, the hand (if it would reach out to me), the axis and position of the head (if it was engaged) . . . I searched for clues to anticipate what she would tell me. If the result of the test was benign or malignant. There was no clue, only her words.

"I'm glad you went for a second opinion because it is malignant."

I shut my eyes and saw absolute black, no lines of red or purple, pure black. My agitation lifted me off the table and I started walking around the examining room in small steps, working off the tension. I thought I might put my fist through the wall.

And then, when I opened my eyes, I couldn't see too well. Or hear too well either. Anna, my good friend who was with me, took the notes, handled the paperwork, received the forms for the additional tests, escorted me through the distorted corridors of the hospital, and finally drove me home, in my brand-new car, my first new car, that no one else but Sandy had driven.

How to see what is there. Simply. Plainly. Without denial. Everything is about seeing and how to see. What to see. Knowing what you are looking at. Figuring out its meaning. Biopsies, machines, micro-scopes—how to see it all in terms of diagnosis and prognosis.

Some diagnostics are as elementary as palpation—touching a lymph node lightly and sensing its swollen form. Other tests require that my body be illuminated by radioactive materials so that my inner parts glow on a screen, making computerized images. Imagism. Imagistics.

Then, with this data, they chart and classify me. On another level, knowing the pathological process, what predictions of related symptoms will be generated? How does the doctor know if there are micro-metastases in my body? The doctor doesn't. It's all supersonic, frontier electronics, perpetrated on this still stone-age human form.

The point is that I am going to die earlier than I should have because of medical incompetence. Today, I have a stage-three breast cancer, which gives me a survival time of between five and eight years. It has already travelled far into my system. But statistical evidence is so crazy anyhow. There are so many individual differences that comparability of cases is strained, if not forced. How many people who received exactly the same protocols responded exactly the same way? But my training is to see generalities, tendencies, and trends, not individual cases, and I must learn this new logic of individual cases, remissions, recoveries, and miracles.

Sandy
February 22

I am on my way home. Barbara has cancer. It is fast-growing and may have already spread to her lymph nodes. More testing, then a mastectomy. I lie here in a hotel in Winnipeg, my mind skittering away from it, "it" being somewhere between mastectomy and death. I make lists in the hopes that what I do will matter.

Is it that I fear the worst at once, or is the worst scenario neces-sary so that I can handle the simpler eventualities? I remember Deena Metzger's story about writing the *Book of Hags*. In December of 1976, she completed her exploration about the nature and function of cancer attacking the breasts of so many young women. What did it mean and why was this the form it took? Only weeks later, she was diagnosed, her own breast having been invaded by cancer. How did she know to prepare for her own battle? How does the subject matter present itself for exploration? Do the fears announce themselves as preparation for reality? When does "knowing" begin?

I want so desperately to engage with Barbara, with this disease, in a loving and useful way. Yet in my racing to strategize and to plan—I lose all feeling. I cannot yet know what this will mean and only hear the terror in her voice.

Barbara
March 7

Exactly one week and three hours after I learned I had cancer, I had a meeting in our house of twenty women who would be involved in my healing and caretaking. It was a conscious and deliberate choice to mobilize a battalion of friends to help and assist me in every phase of fighting my disease. When the doctor told me I had cancer, I was forced to stand alone on a ledge so steep and so scary that I reached out my hand and grabbed the outstretched hands of the women who form my community.

I assembled them so I could tell them all at once of my illness. Oddly, because I am a teacher, I found myself making notes as if for a lecture. I outlined what I needed from them. I listed the concrete ways Sandy and I would need help. It was all neatly categorized and outlined, listed as I would for an introductory class. Being the center of attention was an unusual experience for me and I was nervous and began to read uncomfortably from my notes. Torn between my usual feeling of wanting to be competent and feeling grateful for the room so full of love and concern, after a while I found myself no longer needing my notes, for my heart began to speak. Without censure or artifice, the words found themselves.

I began by sharing the basic information about my cancer and the treatment plan I had chosen to pursue. As I began to hear myself speak, I became aware of how I was lingering on the medical information as a way to postpone saying the more deeply felt words that were in my heart. As I watched their faces react to my words, as well as to the silences between them, I came to understand that I am only the first among our friends to have cancer. There will be others. As the graphs and statistics show, we will hear about more cases as we grow older. Such a weighty responsibility, to be the first, yet it gave me a purpose. I am trying to live self-consciously (and perhaps die self-consciously) in an exemplary manner. Many of my friends will see their future in the way I handle mine.

I told them that I needed to feel useful and to be needed. They spoke of their feelings and their love for me, of their commitment to the shared struggle of winning the battle against the cancer growing in my body, and of their dedication to whatever was needed to win that battle.

That night changed the way I spoke. Since then, many friends have reminded me of my own words:

"Your life is not a rehearsal. It is what it is and you must live it.

"Don't wait to finish your novel to have a baby.

"The days when you want to get dressed up, look outrageous, put those gold earrings on to teach a class, do it. Do it all. There is no time to worry if you are too dressed up to go to work. Do it.

"The restaurant you want to go to but is slightly too expensive. Do it and put it on a credit card.

"Those orchestra tickets for the opera you've always wanted, but you've sat in the balcony because you are saving for a rainy day—buy the orchestra seats.

"The trip you wanted to take but you were waiting until next year. Do it. You might not have next year. Do it now. Do it all. Live your dreams. Live them."

Sandy
Same day

I see her emotional vulnerability, the trembling of her chin when she speaks publicly. She acknowledges my greater ease with the public self by whispering to me before the women gathered, "This is like my first keynote speech," referring to the speeches I make regularly as part of my work. Her late awareness of the love, respect, and concern she generates is unfamiliar; she cannot quite trust these feelings. She simply has no frame of reference for them. I, too, found myself caught in old forms and patterns. After she spoke, I found myself being charming, gracious, welcoming—all the social skills I use without thinking. Appalled at the ease with which such forms blot out feelings, I just as unexpectedly began to cry and spoke publicly, perhaps for the first time, utterly without charm, grace or style. From my heart.

Barbara
Same day

After I was finished speaking, I was asked to stretch out on the floor and the women gathered in a circle around me, each of them laying hands upon my body. Rituals and those who practice them are strange to me, but it felt soothing and I could hear the sounds of women weeping and feel energy being passed from their bodies to mine.

Earlier in the day I had spoken to Deena in Los Angeles who suggested I find a visualization for the moment when the chemotherapy enters my body for the first time. I asked the women in my healing circle to visualize the same image at the time of the injection/invasion. It was to be at 4 p.m. on Monday. As I lay upon the floor, encircled by their bodies, their hands, and their love, I began to sense the power of such a suggestion.

The chemotherapy that will be used is the strongest currently available, hopefully doing enough to match and conquer the formidable enemy that has invaded me. There is going to be a war waged inside my body and I will need support, nurturance, caring, diversion, laughter, and safety to endure the eighteen months that lie ahead. These twenty women and others across the country will serve as my companions.

Sandy
Same day

Now that the house has emptied, the images that keep intruding are those of a malevolent circus. The kind in the movies of the '40s where the final chase scene takes place on a carousel gone mad with the chilling voice of the laughing fat woman as seen through the mirrors of the fun house. My images are those of tightropes I must walk to keep balanced between my life and ours. Juggling to keep us distinct yet joined. The speed with which the disease is growing in her body like a roller coaster out of control. My moods are wide-ranging and unpredictable. I marvel at her. I marvel at me. And sometimes I want her to tell me she's sorry for getting cancer and ruining our lives together. And sometimes I'm angry at her for getting it. Other times I want to tell her that I am sorry for letting her get cancer and not making her go to a better doctor. And most of the time, I lie in her arms grateful for the life we have together.

Sandy
March 9

The medical procedures began today. Barbara had a needle biopsy in the morning that confirmed a cancerous node in her neck. This underscores the need for chemotherapy first, before surgery.

Later that same day, no time to wait now, she had her first course of chemotherapy. I called all the women in our support network and asked them to visualize, at the precise moment the infusion was scheduled, the chemotherapy entering her body and moving through her bloodstream to destroy the cancerous cells. I felt a bit shy and awkward about making such a request, but I'm willing to try anything now.

As Barbara sat stiffly on a chair in the doctor's treatment room, I knelt beside her. My hand rested on her lap, and I imaged like crazy, determined my energy would join the chemotherapy to fight this disease. The process went on interminably, fat syringes filled with clear blue and red liquids. First one was slowly emptied into Barbara's arm as she stared unblinkingly at it, then another, yet another—her breathing growing shallow, anxious. When it was over, the needle mercifully withdrawn, we fled, grateful, eager to return home.

Barbara
March 12

Whew! The worst of the chemo reaction is over. Nonstop vomiting for two days. I've lost seven pounds. It was intense and, in moments, grim. My throat went into spasm from all that vomiting. Just swallowing hurt.

And now I have mouth sores and feel scared about radiation. How much of a decrease in energy will there be? How much pain? The next ten weeks of physical hardship seem almost unendurable, unbearable. I look at my arm, thin and bruised from the chemotherapy injections, and feel pity for myself.

I tossed and turned all night. I was restless, got up, ate, went back to bed, got up for an allergy pill, went back to bed. I finally got up and went into another room at four-thirty. When I couldn't place myself in a comfortable position, couldn't get my body to fit and be still, my mind flashed forward to some uncertain time in the future when bone metastases might really prevent me from getting comfortable.

I'm very fearful now. Fearful that the cancer will spread. Of radiation. Of recurrence. Fearful about pain, restlessness, weakness, dependency. I sit here at dawn and my mind races forward and backward.

Sandy
March 15

Today we went downtown to buy a wig. Barbara sat in the salon chair, angrily pulling on wig after wig, making bad jokes, growing anxious, then after less than an hour, she became too tired to continue and was ready to return home. As we walked to the car she leaned heavily on my arm, the way my mother, now in her seventies, does.

She is asleep now and I feel drained. Fourteen days ago I heard the words, and only now do I begin to understand what they may mean.

Sandy
March 19

Barbara is weak from the effects of chemotherapy and spends much of her time in bed now, alternately reading and sleeping. I, too, am sleeping more than usual, my nights filled with horrifying dreams that thankfully evaporate when I awaken.

Barbara
March 20

Sandy and I watched *Gypsy* last night and we both wept. I'm not sure why, but I think it was something about Rose's powerlessness in the face of her daughter's choices. Or perhaps we both just needed to cry and anything would have generated it.

I went alone today to see Dr. Grant for my post-chemotherapy visit. This painful disentangling is necessary for both of us. The truth is that it is not our cancer but mine. I have to find my way alone now.

Barbara
March 26

Every day I have a race with the bottle of shampoo I bought the day chemotherapy began. Will my hair all fall out by the time the shampoo is finished or will it outlast me? Sometimes I look at my dog, who is now eight years old, and say out loud, "I'm going to outlive you!"

Barbara
March 28

What a terrific day I had. The second cycle of chemotherapy began and my nodes are down fifty percent. Yippee! The consultation I had with the oncological surgeon confirms Dr. Grant's treatment plan of three cycles of chemotherapy before the mastectomy. I feel wonderful about all of this. I also took this chemo better. I'm still very fatigued but there was less nausea. I had a good time with friends—dinner and interesting talk. Good for me! I feel like singing and jumping. I'm getting to be my happy self again.

Barbara's first letter to the support group
March 29

Dear Friends,

Enclosed is the schedule for my coverage during the second chemo week while Sandy is away.

For most of the time during the first few days I will be sleeping, so please bring things that will keep you busy. It might be helpful to check in with the person who will be with me before your shift in case there are things you need to pick up.

The most important thing for me is to have ice cubes by my bed and to drink lots of fluids. I am using organic produce and foods only. Grapefruits, carrots, apples, and greens constitute most of my juice diet. I also eat eggs, cereal, and salads with sprouts.

The freezer will be well stocked with organic ice pops and sherbets, but check to see if the supply is getting low.

I would appreciate it very much if you could walk the dog during your shift.

Finally, please answer the phone (which will be unplugged in my bedroom) and make a note of all messages. Either Sandy or I will return calls when we can. If my parents call (they do not yet know that I have cancer), please give a cheerful response that indicates nothing is wrong.

You all have my thanks and appreciation for your willingness to help me and Sandy.

Love,

Barbara

Sandy
March 30

I am in Duluth facilitating a workshop for counselors who work with survivors of sexual abuse. Meanwhile, in San Francisco, streams of women move through our home, responding to Barbara's letter for help. I continue to work because I don't know what else to do. It is so much an integral part of who I am. Without it I feel diminished—less able to be the woman Barbara fell in love with. Less able to nourish and help her in this time.

I have to learn to allow others to help us, to do some of the caregiving. Yet I still feel torn and guilty at the relief I feel to be back in my own life for a few days. I call home every four hours to be sure each woman has shown up for her shift, that there are no unforeseen symptoms, and that Barbara is in good spirits.

She is losing her hair. Next month she will lose a breast. It makes the cancer less an intellectual reality and more concrete, more physical.

I worry about how I will negotiate the high wire of self and other. Autonomy and engagement. Commitment and absence. How will her cancer force me to engage with the choices of being both in my life and in hers as well—and still keep my balance?

Barbara's forty-second birthday
April 9

Dear Friends,

There has been such a tremendous outpouring of letters, cards, flowers, and love that it has already made an enormous difference in my strength, courage and healing. I thank you all. The number of caring people in my life requires me to put information in this form, so please don't take offense at its impersonality.

First, the diagnosis: I have "advanced" breast cancer, which requires an eighteen-month treatment plan. "Advanced" means that the lymph system is involved. I'm already on a strong form of chemotherapy and I'll be having it for three months. Then a mastectomy of the right breast, followed by three additional months of chemotherapy. Then radiation of the breast area to make sure the area is "sterilized," that is, no small cancer cells exist. And then I'll be on a different kind of chemotherapy for another year at a dosage and schedule that is less aggressive than the first six months.

Already the chemotherapy is making a difference. The bumps and lumps in my Iymph system have been reduced by fifty percent following the first cycle. Following the second, the tumor size in the breast is also reduced by almost fifty percent. Chemotherapy consists of injections of deadly chemicals into the body and there are notorious side effects. Luckily for me, I'm taking it extremely well, with a minimum of bad effects.

My spirit and courage are strong and I am prepared for a long fight in many, many ways. Friends have remarked that I'm doing well and I feel, for the most part, good and extraordinarily happy to be alive. One fight I'm waging is a malpractice suit against Kaiser Hospital, which failed to diagnose my tumor as cancer over a year ago. They dismissed it, time after time, as benign fibrocystic disease.

Their incompetence fills me with rage and tremendous sadness because early detection was a real possibility and failed to happen. Like many things in life, this is something I am coming to accept slowly, but not without profound emotional feeling. However, I am currently receiving state-of-the-art medical care and am regaining some trust in the medical establishment. I am optimistic that over the next five or ten years, more advances will be made and that I will benefit from them.

My life is very different now. I have an intense awareness and adolescentlike emotional sensitivity. I find myself comforted by poetry, chamber music, and being in the natural world. I have been too anxious to be able to read cerebral stuff, including sociology, and, frankly, lots of things in life look like bullshit to me, including many of the things I thought were dear and important. I have been thrown into a crisis of meaning and I am searching for different answers to my life, which now has a sense of finiteness. Time is incredibly important, and, every month, I do something I always wanted to do but, somehow, never found the time. Tomorrow, Sandy and I are going to Anza-Borrego, a desert near San Diego, to see the cactus in bloom. Next month we'll have another adventure before surgery. And after the eighteen months of treatment, perhaps a trip around the world.

Because I am so aware of time, I want to live richly and fully, and do a great many things during the next years of my life. People, closeness, laughter, good times, trips, connectedness with friends and nature, music, and poetry. Right now, these are important. If I write something, it will probably be to be useful to other women who will have this experience. Somehow, I need to be of use and I need to write something that will help others, in addition to solving interesting intellectual problems.

I am doing everything I can to get my immune system working again: a special diet for cancer patients, relaxation, visualization, and all forms of healing, both conventional and alternative. Love and caring are very much part of how I live and I want you to know how important your caring is to me. It is part of what gives me strength and meaning. I'll write again after surgery. All of you, take care of yourselves. And take the time to be alive every day and every minute.

With love,

Barbara

Sandy's forty-seventh birthday
April 19

I have spent the past few days writing notes to friends, helping Barbara answer some of her well-wishers and as a consequence I find my own thoughts greatly clarified. Finding simpler ways to say complex things. Barbara is responding well to chemotherapy; her tumor is shrinking considerably and the nodes under her arm are hardly palpable. Consequently she may have another round of chemotherapy before surgery so that the mass is as small as possible. We are both greatly heartened by this news.

We continue to enjoy each other in a thousand small ways. The companionable dependencies, the knowledge of small habits, the playful rituals are all grounding and provide the sense of continuity that mocks the disease. And there is even the passion. Less frequent. Quite unexpected. But during our four days in the tenacious and dogged landscape of Anza-Borrego, when the desert was in bloom, it entered and took us over. For a few days we were deliberate and

21

intent upon our bodies. Not as the genesis of disease, of potential loss, of mortality. During that peaceful respite from the exhausting emotional maelstrom of our lives, flesh was generative, a cause of tears and rejoicing.

Today, on my forty-seventh birthday, I am full in my heart and grateful for my life in all its complexities.

Class Travel

Sandy

We plan quiet weekends. Just the two of us closing ranks to prepare for what the months ahead will bring. We take long walks followed by dinner at one of our favorite restaurants. Last night Barbara ordered something unfamiliar—a dozen assorted oysters—tasting each one with the focused intensity she brings to all new experience.

The shock has worn off a bit but I am still frightened. It took so many years for me to allow my dependence on her, but now that I have, I feel desperate not to lose her.

The first of a series of tests has begun, and I insist upon being in the room as they place her on a metal table and wheel her into a tunnel-like apparatus, while the machines slowly and inexorably move up and back over the length of her body. She lies so still on the table, not moving, as she was instructed.

I stare at the screen producing color images that I cannot decipher. A young man sits immobile before it making notes. I cannot see what he writes and cannot tell from his posture or expression if there is danger on the screen.

She avoids looking at me, just stares up at the ceiling as my eyes race around the room trying to understand the technology, the stillness. In one corner a young intern reads the daily paper. In another, a doctor makes notes on her chart for the staff. Everywhere there is silence. I would speak to Barbara but cannot imagine what to say. I hope my presence is of help to her. It isn't to me. I feel superfluous. Helpless.

There are so many dangerous possibilities. So many symptoms. A lump under her armpit may mean further spread. Tendonitis may mean metastasis to the bone. Dizziness—it may be the brain. A sore throat may be symptomatic of cancer of the larynx. Endless possibilities and now, as I stand over her, they all seem ominous.

Then we sit and wait for the results in an empty room. Again, I cannot imagine what to say. My hand does not move to reach out to her. I am encased in my own terror and cannot join her in her own. Like the staff in the examining room, we sit side by side without moving, in silence.

"Everything seems just fine," we are finally told. "No further spread that we can see." We turn to each other then, our hands reach to touch and we allow ourselves to breathe. We celebrate that small victory with an expensive dinner. At least, we reassure ourselves and each other, it is only what it is. It isn't more.

Our level of tension is cyclical. Laughter and tears blend, our moods are unexpected, unpredictable. My desire to protect her is sometimes overwhelming.

I am aware of needing to find a balance between my need to protect her—to throw myself across her to keep the cancer away— and respecting her need to proceed through this experience as she needs to, allowing all the people in her life to love her and not letting myself be in the way. My own sense of balance eludes me now and I stumble.

Barbara

Sandy goes with me for all the tests. We've been together for six years, and yet she sometimes feels like a stranger to me. She has been unusually quiet during these last few days of testing. They put me into machines; Sandy sits in a chair nearby. Watching. She cannot ask them to stop the test, to comfort me. We sit together in one waiting room after the other with long silences and yellow pads. It seems the only stuff worth talking about is the medical information.

Words just hang there, become useless. They are revealed as clumsy instruments of communication so she, and I, are mute. Dumb. This woman of so many words, so many verbal styles, presentations, public speeches is mute with me. And that is how I know—in part—how deadly serious this is. We cannot use words to build bridges between us, as we have done in the past. We are each trapped in our own terror and cannot find our way towards each other.

Sandy

It wasn't until the skin around her nipple began to pucker that she grew frightened and called from New York asking me to arrange for an examination with a doctor outside the Kaiser system. I scheduled an appointment with an older, established, woman physician affiliated with a prestigious hospital. That was the turning point for Barbara, I think. That was the point at which she began gathering information outside the public health system. The shift from public to private was a major one for it took a while for us to understand she had been misdiagnosed. The lump we found in March of 1984 was not diagnosed as cancer until February of 1985. During that time, it grew from two cm to six cm; her breast enlarged to nearly twice its original size. A mammogram that Barbara had demanded be taken was read incorrectly as negative by a radiologist. She saw three doctors and, still, no one was concerned. "It's below the index of suspicion," she had been told by a surgeon at Kaiser, three weeks before she was finally diagnosed. Told she had fibrocystic disease. Told to stop drinking coffee. They would watch it.

The ambivalence she suffers is painful for me. Her overwhelming sense that she should—somehow—have known. That she should have insisted on something. And yet she did everything she could. She did monthly breast self-examinations. She demanded a mammogram when they would not have ordered one. She requested the tests that had not been routinely ordered. She drove herself to be the best consumer she could, in the same way she drives herself to be the best at everything she does.

Once the diagnosis was made, once the cancer was discovered, she began to research obsessively. Chemotherapy first? Surgery first? Radiation with lumpectomy was ruled out. There was a blur of days filled with doctors, examinations, treatment recommendations, yellow pads filled with questions and answers, and Barbara with her pocket tape recorder chronicling each doctor's answers in case she grew too anxious and could not hear what was being said.

Barbara

And then there is another problem: the differences in the recommendations given by different specialists. Surgeons tend to see breast cancer as a local disease, so they want to cut first. Oncologists see cancer systemically, as an immune system disease, and they say attack with chemotherapy. Then, when I went to see three different oncologists, I got three different opinions anyhow; it threw me into a crisis of uncertainty.

Now I make lists of questions, gather up my tape recorder and am lucid, direct, insistent, and clear in my repeated interviews with the series of private "experts" Sandy and I now consult. I have finally chosen an oncologist, a tough-minded woman, and developed a treatment plan. The "best." A "top man," as my mother would say. Chemotherapy first. Then surgery. Then more chemotherapy. Then radiation. Then more chemotherapy. It is a very aggressive treatment with devastating side effects: loss of hair, vomiting, prematurely induced menopause, fatigue; but it seems the only chance of controlling this virulent force that has invaded my body.

Medicine offers no certainty but I must trust someone. Dr. Kathy Grant is a tough, gentle, sensitive, coolly professional woman, a few years younger than me. She will be my lifeline. She will become the center of my life. I will visit her for a year and a half for my treatments. I will fall in love with her, hold on to her every word, her every hope for me. I will turn to her for optimism, realism, help, understanding, drugs. She is my doctor, my hope, my survival.

I just completed filing a malpractice suit with an attorney because a series of incompetent doctors failed to make an accurate diagnosis of my breast cancer. I hate them but I'm also filled with self-loathing, self-doubt. What should I have done? Why didn't I insist upon something? Why didn't I know better? But I never learned to recognize a good doctor. Public medicine was all I had ever experienced. Despite my "class travel," I still went to clinics, just as I had when I was ten, waiting for my glasses to be given to me for free.

Often now, when I go to the doctor, I remember my father. When he was eleven, two years before his *bar mitzvah*, he became an apprentice to what is called in Polish/Yiddish a *feldsher*. While there is no adequate translation for this phrase, my father says it could be translated as "paramedic" or "country doctor." When he talks about *feldshers* in an unselfconscious way, he calls them half-doctors. A *feldsher* was a government-certified, somewhat-trained, medical person who did the following: placed leeches for bloodletting; applied heated cups to lacerations made on the back in order to draw blood; pulled teeth; lanced and then filled abscesses with iodized gauze. He was in charge of the health of local villagers, and when there was an eruption of even one case of a contagious disease, such as what my father calls in Yiddish *scarletina* (scarlet fever), he would report it to the authorities of the local medical district. My father was a *feldsher's* apprentice and, had he remained in Europe, would have probably become a *feldsher* himself.

All my life I believed that, if I became ill, I would go on the subway to the hospital, wait patiently to see the doctor, and be appreciative of the small hurried bits of time they proffered. This was the only experience I ever had. Mass medicine was for the mass of people—I was one of the masses. I never had a private physician, never had been to a private hospital. Never to a lawyer's office. Now I go to the Heads of Departments; the Chief of Oncology refers me to the Head of Radiology and the Head of Surgery, and they spend time with me. Not the HMO's quota of one patient every twelve minutes. I never deeply understood that class was a matter of life and death.

My class. My life.

Ruffled Iris

May – July 1985

Barbara
May 12

The night before the mastectomy. A pizza party with my best girlfriends. Fun, laughter, practicality, sadness. Lots of medical stories.

I've handled lots of my scared feelings. The closer it gets to the actual hour, the more steady I become. Saying all the hard things, facing all the hard feelings. I'm ready to be cut.

Barbara
May 15, 5 a.m.

IN THE HOSPITAL. The exact number of nodes is unimportant. I am beyond that, the doctors say. For some women there are breaking points, zero to four, four to ten. But now they tell me that the cancer's spread into my lymph system is too advanced for this to be meaningful. I interpret this in terms of worst-case scenarios. Five to eight years to live.

I'm scared again. Now that the surgery is over, the next steps revolve around quality-of-life issues. If there's any chance to help kill the cancer, it must be taken. Any diet, experimental techniques, every chance.

Sandy
May 15

She will never get well. Barbara is going to die. It is now only a matter of years. I repeat this new reality over and over, much as I did the original diagnosis. Barbara has cancer. She has had cancer. Her cancer is advanced and will be terminal. Hello. This is Sandy. I'm calling with some upsetting news. Barbara has advanced breast cancer.

Such knowledge requires repetition to become real. Not just the words. But what it will mean in her body. In our lives. I feel cold inside and immerse myself in the immediacy of what has to be done so I don't let myself feel. I want to bury my head in her lap and weep. Shake my fist at the heavens.

I have spent the past ten years of my life writing and talking, training and facilitating so that women can speak and engage both politically and psychologically with all the forms of violence against women. Now, this violence against this woman leaves me frozen and silent.

Sandy
May 18

I sat beside Barbara during the five days she spent in the hospital recovering from the mastectomy, monitoring each nap, each shot, each walk down the long, polished corridor. My presence beside her was the reassurance I needed. It wasn't until she returned home that I realized how little she remembered of those sedated days.

I was prepared for how Barbara would look after her surgery because I have a copy of the poster Deena Metzger made after her mastectomy: where she is nude and exuberantly leaping into the air. I remember too one long-ago afternoon in Deena's home in Los Angeles, as she lifted her blouse over her head to show me her newly shaped body. There was a tree of life tattooed over her scar, her chest now "an illuminated manuscript."

Now, Deena has sent us a small crocus pot with a note saying that it reminded her of Barbara's delicate sensibility, of her love of small ruffled irises. Kissing Barbara in the hospital, my mouth moving along the ruffled skin of her scar brought tears to both our eyes. She is bald now from the chemo, but her head looks beautiful and she has a quality of elegance that has always escaped her before.

Barbara
May 20

I no longer have the energy I once had. Planning dates, appointments, even a movie with a friend, has become problematic. It's hard to know how I'll feel until exactly that day or moment. Appointment-making is now conditional; everything I plan is contingent on how I feel. People are good about that and seem to understand that I sometimes need to cancel or change plans at the last minute.

There are two sources of my fatigue. First, the post-surgical recovery would be enough for anybody to deal with. But on top of surgery, I got light doses of chemotherapy. Fatigue is hard; things feel overwhelming. I get frustrated, whiny, and irritated. I need to sleep every afternoon, sometimes twice, like a young child. I can't count on my body, my energy, my level of concentration or my ability to remember.

Loss of memory was the first post-diagnostic psychological symptom I noticed. Names, places, time, events eluded me. My cancer counselor told me that forgetting was the most prevalent symptom among people with cancer. It is, she said, the mind's way to protect you from experiencing the terror of knowing.

The same thing is true of my inability to concentrate. I can hardly pay attention to anything for longer than ten minutes before unbidden, intrusive thoughts take me away into my fears and fantasies, into a world of worry about sickness and death.

Everything is affected. My internal life is now episodically constructed and the episodes are briefer. My day is a string of short events, linked together by a sense of continuity. What used to be a day that seemed to have three groups of four hours each has now become fifty brief encounters. I can't sustain long-term energy or focus.

Chemotherapy also distorts time. My chemotherapy consists of three drugs, each of which is calibrated to peak on different days. In my case, one works on the fifth day after the infusion, the second on day fourteen, and the third works continuously in small cycles of fluctuation. Recovery from each cycle of chemotherapy, then, is not like recovery from a cold. With a cold, each day offers some percentage of improvement over the previous one. But, during chemo, days one and two are miserable, filled with vomiting and nausea. There's relief on days three and four and a bit less fatigue than the first two days; and then, boom, day five kicks in, and the awful mouth sores start, and the fatigue begins. I have to tolerate horrible side effects from the drugs, the inside of my mouth becomes inflamed and sore, and then the symptoms lift a bit. No sooner do I have a day of relief than day fourteen comes and the third drug peaks, bringing new symptoms with it. This cycle is repeated every twenty-one days, and days nineteen, twenty and twenty-one are the best—after the peak effects have passed—when I'm recovered the most.

Some people say that I don't know anything about exhaustion now—just wait until radiation. Perhaps, but at least I won't have systemic symptoms like mouth sores and nausea.

My intelligence is intact but refocused. I attempt to harness it in the service of a task, but it drifts to what it needs, mostly information about cancer, like a water finder. I attempt to subject my body to the will of my mind and am unsuccessful. I try to keep alert, force myself to pay attention, take this situation by the horns, make my body cooperate. But, alas, at noon today, only three and a half hours after I left home to go to my office, I'm back in bed sleeping. My body has needs of its own and no single act of will can make it do other.

Prediction and routine are intertwined. What has become routinized can be counted on, predicted from. My routines are radically altered and interrupted. Fatigue leads me to walk in a shuffle—step by step. It feels like I weigh a ton. I walk into furniture, less sure-footed and competent.

Sandy
June 4

I am leaving for Canada for two weeks to give a series of workshops for activist women. Both Barbara's sister Ruth and her childhood friend Stan are here. Her parents will arrive next week. I feel displaced and jealous of her intimacy with them. All the old rough and unresolved places of our relationship resurface. All the tangled threads of her specific history that exclude me. But at the same time, I am released. Reprieved. Able to be in my own life for a week or so. To remember myself.

Barbara
June 6

Today I bought a $3,000 stereo system. I can't believe I did it. There is a distinctly unreal quality to this, but it's everything I've always wanted and more. It's funny how the threat of dying intensifies the need to live—and to live fully and hugely, to devour everything. Music, art, ideas, everything. There's so little time, it seems. Even if it's ten years, that's not enough. Not even twenty years would be.

Having Ruth and Stan here, buying and installing the stereo, overshadows most everything. I can't remember being happier with them and with many parts of myself. How boundless is the love I have for Ruth! How wonderful she is! Sensitive, with delicate yet strong sensibilities, warm, caring, observant, nurturant: she's terrific. And Stan, what wonderful love I have for him. A brother, and more, a friend. How lucky I am to be so loved!

Even this tiny little fuzz that grew back on my head as a consequence of not having chemotherapy for a few weeks makes me feel less vulnerable, less exposed, my head covered in the presence of God and life. But it will soon fall from my head again and I will have to go through it yet another time—these little loose hairs departing from me.

Stan, his friend Ceil, and I talked about cremation. They're both going to do it but I still feel strongly about the interdiction that Jews should leave the same way we arrived. In Jewish law, a person must leave with the same body, no alterations, no cremation. But now I can't count on my body to be the same through time. Does mastectomy count? Is my body the same?

Barbara
June 11

My mother and father are here. What excitement, stimulation! It's amazing I love them so much. In just the first five minutes—the joy of a family reunion and concern from both parents, all mixed with the usual animated talk about politics.

Last night, while sitting at the kitchen table, my father asked the meaning of an unfamiliar word in the *New York Times*. I told him, feeling great pleasure and delight at this seventy-four-year-old man's desire to learn new things. His love of words. How like mine!

Ruth and I had what will probably be the first of many conversations about her inheritance from my will and the role I hope Sandy will play in her life after I die. I cried when talking about Sandy, the ways in which she can be a friend, an advisor, and like family. She's a good and loving person, and I want Ruth not to feel abandoned and alone. In my living, and even now in my dying, still protecting and taking care of.

I'm almost manic from all the stimulation and my alternating swings from despair to optimism. I can sleep only five hours at a time and am needing to take Valium every night. When Sandy returns from Halifax on Saturday, I will rely on her norm-setting, rule-enforcing disposition to get me back on a normal sleeping schedule.

Sandy is the archetypal mother. She tends and supervises. As much as I resent and complain about it, I haven't taken a real nap since she's gone. Deep relaxation yes, but no sleep. Her presence allows me to come to rest.

Barbara
June 12

It's been confirmed—what I had feared all along. Today I learned that my mammogram had been read wrong by the radiologist at Kaiser. It showed there had been cancer from my first visit. I'm completely numb.

I know that people make mistakes all the time. Secretaries make typos; business people make bad judgments; even I made serious goof-ups in my job of the last five years. But this mistake is my life. My cancer was misdiagnosed by several doctors, all at the same medical facility, more than one year before it was finally diagnosed as cancer. Even when one breast was one and a half times the size of the other, no one was suspicious enough to do a needle biopsy. They just said to stay off caffeine for a while. I'm usually very smart but I got lost in their system and feel betrayed by their incompetence.

The task of being the competent one in my family fell on my shoulders. My parents are poor European immigrants, with little education, little savvy in the world of business, little ability to plan for the future and implement those plans. They have always concerned themselves with the daily business of survival: shopping, preparing food, keeping clean, sleeping enough for work the next day.

From the time I was small, the task of explaining to them how the world worked fell to me. I didn't know much, but I observed. I became competent in school, in reading, in the ways people behaved. Over the years, I constantly added new skills to my areas of competence. I became a fine teacher and received high evaluations from my students. Then a good writer, book reviewer, thinker, cook, photographer. My present job required me to learn how to be a competent administrator, so I did that too. Whatever I did, I had to be competent at it. It was like a river whose tributaries reached into every aspect of my being. It became a fetish.

But there was one blind spot in my life, in my obsession to excel at everything. Despite my preoccupation with competence, the one thing I failed to learn about was what makes a first-rate doctor.

I never had any idea what constituted a good doctor or good medicine. As a poor child in Brooklyn, I obtained medical treatment in clinics. I waited for long hours on hard benches for my bureaucratically assigned number to be called on the anonymous loudspeaker system. I never knew a doctor could spend more than ten minutes with a patient. I became used to shoddy medicine and believed that the hurried mass medicine I received was the medical standard. I was done in by medical incompetence. I also failed as an expert on myself. I failed because I didn't know that the doctors weren't good. I didn't know they didn't order the right tests. They failed me and I failed myself. This is a tragic farce of failures and betrayal. And, in the end, I will die an early death because I was not competent enough to discern and judge the incompetence of my doctors. And this, for a woman who spent so much time trying to become competent at everything, is the ultimate irony.

Barbara
June 13

Before my breast was removed, my cancer counselor gave me a body image test. My score was high. I liked my body as a whole and all its parts.

I checked off "very satisfied" when asked how I liked my nose, eyes, mouth. And my hips, breasts, thighs. Well, my calves are quite thick, and I suppose I could be a bit more thin-waisted, but all in all I liked my body. It was pleasurable and adequate.

Then there was the surgery and the aftershock of watching the surgeon remove one by one the staples like train tracks where my breast had been. The first time I looked at my chest, I was horrified. I touched myself at least twenty-five times a day, looking for my breast. But it wasn't there anymore.

Then I took the body image test again, but this time I hated my body: my waist, thighs, hips. I hated my hairlessness. The loss of my breast made the earlier pain, humiliation, and the embarrassment of losing my hair almost unbearable. Now, my pubic hair has come back for a short time, until the next chemo causes it to fall out again. Chemo also works on my upper lip hair as well, one macabre side effect that's positive.

I have also come to understand that who you vomit with is more important than who you have sex with. Right now I can only vomit with two people, Sandy and Ruth, and feel comfortable. Yes, I have humiliation and powerlessness but it's tolerable. But I could probably have sex with twenty people. So what? Which is more important?

This is a time for courage, bravery, steadfastness, conviction, valor, and a belief that I will be cured. But I'm in despair. I miss Sandy. Ten days is a long time.

Barbara
June 14

I took care of myself today. Instead of calling up Kathy Grant to get the estrogen receptor results, I decided to wait until Monday, when Sandy is home and we can handle whatever it is together. A reprieve for the weekend and not having to create a false self for my visiting parents.

I've been very depressed today, fusing several losses into one unmanageable one. Ruth's going back to New York makes me weepy. Separation is so hard. And Sandy's not being here feels terrible now, as opposed to the liberation of the first week.

Now everything feels like loss. And I ask myself, "Who would want me now?" I don't think I have the energy to open up my heart to anyone. One more person to say good-bye to. And who would want to be friends with me? I'm going to leave them.

Sandy
June 15

HALIFAX. Intense days of work, homogeneous and interchangeable hotel rooms, moving through long airport corridors late at night. I am here to provide respite for front-line activists, exhausted, overwhelmed with the avalanche of violence they respond to: rape, battered women, abused children. These women struggle with burnout, and I provide a two day workshop called Healing the Healers, a process I offer, a process I need for myself.

Ruth has just left. She felt like an ally to me, someone who knew what to do. Now just her parents are there, themselves needing protection and care. Barbara sounded anxious on the phone last night, waiting for me to return home before getting the estrogen receptor results. She is discouraged as she comes to understand the incompetence surrounding her past medical care and the way her life has been shortened by it.

I long for everything to return to normal, back to the way it all was before, before this cancer became the centerpiece around which we now live. I imagine myself placing a lacy shawl across the bony mask of death, murmuring to it, "Not yet. It is not time. You will gather her back, as you gather us all. She will not elude you. None of us ever do. Don't frighten her. She still has time and is not ready to join you." Sometimes I can even imagine the mask's grimace soften and change shape, becoming a bowl of freshly cut ruffled irises from the bulbs Barbara has planted.

Barbara
June 18

I am having one of those "if only" days. "If only" I had gone to a women's clinic. "If only" I had better doctors. "If only" I had described my symptoms to friends more. "If only. If only." I grew up in a house where we talked about the quality of meat, but never the quality of doctors. All doctors were the same. There were no hierarchies among them. No differences.

Today I feel my death sentence painfully. Today I tell myself that my cancer is really a stage four, not a stage three. Today I tell myself the truth—no bullshit. Today my life shortens even more in front of my eyes.

I have been professionally trained to deal with observation and interpretation. I'm fascinated by seeing and by what conditions and structures what we see. How we see. I'm good at seeing. I'm even better at seeing through and below surface manifestations to inner patterns, inner structure and design. More important: inner meanings·and external interpretations.

I was blind for a year, surrounded by other blind people. Except they have no excuse. I hate them.

I'm terrified of getting the estrogen receptor results. Sandy is out with the dog and I'm afraid to be alone. I have avoided making the call to the doctor for the past six days. I can't bear it now. It feels like trembling into death. The time grows shorter and shorter, retracting like a turtle's head.

Where is Sandy? Why doesn't she rush home and throw open the front door: the dog will yelp, the world will be changed, miracles performed. I try to communicate how scared I am to Sandy but I feel so incredibly alone. Her arms don't comfort me. I feel like I'm looking down death's throat and will be swallowed within five years. My own sense of time shrinks every day and is amplified by my mother's presence, the heavy weight of her despair and suffering.

My parents are in my hair (or would be if I had any!), getting in the way, sticky. Their constant talk about food drives me nuts and today I have little patience. I badly need to be taken care of. I want Sandy to help me cope but it feels like she can't help me. I feel very abandoned and lost.

I have fewer boundaries now. More needs. Our vulnerabilities are not of equal weight. Our needs seem out of sync and out of proportion. Sandy has never seemed more independent, more separate, and I have never been so needy. My sense of time is urgent. Hers seems scattered all over the place. We can't align our priorities, it seems.

Barbara
June 21

A day to remember. Sandy took me and my parents to Prego's for dinner, reminding me of the life force of pasta alfredo and ice cream. Then, home to a videotape of *Carmen* choreographed for flamenco dancers. Since Sandy has devoted more time to me and to my parents, I'm much more able to cope. Things roll right off me.

I'm jealous of her enormous energy. I can't sustain a full day on chemo without sleeping, or at least resting. I love those moments when I forget I have cancer. When I have a good time and am filled with zest and energy.

Sandy
June 22

I am overwhelmed with longing as I observe the direct simplicity with which Barbara's mother and father fill her with loving. Her mother bustling in our kitchen; freshly juiced carrots, roasted chicken, rice pudding, barley soup all lovingly tendered. Shopping creates the structure of their day, each morning organized around a short but necessary list. Two onions, one pepper, some cumin and low fat milk. Ingredients without which the acts of loving cannot begin.

Barbara grows irritated by their lack of organization, but I understand. In a complex, dangerous world, shopping is one activity about which her parents feel confident. Three for $1.89 compared to two for 99 cents. This is the currency of their knowledge and love.

Barbara's father is nearly blind—his eyes magnified with thick glasses as he carefully peels and chops, mixes, stirs. I glimpse Barbara's delicate sensibility as he gently sprinkles small slices of scallions in a careful circle over his egg salad. Barbara sits reading in the living room as her parents work together in our kitchen. Her mother abruptly turns to her and says, "If we thought it would be useful, we would move out of our apartment and live closer to you." Barbara meets her mother's eyes and does not reply.

I know I romanticize these old Jews; I know I too am surrounded by many accepting and openhearted women, but for the moment the quality of such unconditional love fills me with yearning.

Barbara

June 23

I want to squeeze life out of every minute, even if it means being up at dawn to watch the changing light and to listen to the first birds of the day.

Today is the longest day of the year. At 5:30 a.m. it was light, yet still overcast with dull morning tones. The garden is beautiful. Sandy trellised the vine and planted periwinkle for color. The giant marigolds are huge. The tomatoes are coming in now, little green balls everywhere: hard, tiny tomatoes.

My parents left today and I wept. I feel quite sad, even now, twelve hours later. I see so much good in them, so much love, so much trying. A cheerfulness that is quite genuine and an optimism about my health that is almost infectious.

This separation is hard. I feel ripped apart on the inside and weepy now. Part of this has to do with my concealing the seriousness of my diagnosis from my parents—I tell myself they will die before I do and don't need to know.

I'm frightened. Sometimes I wonder why my adjustment to cancer isn't quicker. I'm so damn fast at everything, why does this take so long? When will it become my new reality? When will I relax into it more? I'm not quiet inside, I'm quivering most of the time. Nobody can make it go away, not even Sandy.

I got lost with all these visits and need to find myself in the quiet. I need to sleep alone tonight. Stay close to the bone, focused on nuance, mood. Not respond to Sandy's intense work energy. I had a disturbing dream last night—I was fighting with Sandy. Maybe it's a clue to take a day's break from my dependency that always comes up at chemo time.

Listening to the *Bach Unaccompanied Cello No. 1* on the stereo makes me cry. There's so much beauty, so much gorgeousness in life. The intensity of this feeling makes me weep both for joy and the truth of my shortened years. When I look at myself in the mirror now, my heart breaks. I wonder what I did wrong. Am I being punished?

Sandy
July 10

Barbara has expressed a desire to have quiet time to herself this fall. I understand that the first stage of the two of us huddled together in the face of this disease is winding down. We both want and need to move to a different level of separation. I want Barbara to feel safe and protected by me, while at the same time, I need to feel engaged with my own life in a daily way. I'm preparing to rent office space to use for a few hours each day, buy a computer, begin work on a short piece for an anthology. All small steps that generate guilt, uncertainty, and confusion in me, but some welcome distance as well. It's time for us to find a different way forward.

Sandy
July 13

Barbara has been feeling strong for the past day and a half and is filled with energy to grow new life in her garden. She wears vegetable earrings in that splendidly whimsical way she has. Bald, with carrots dangling from her ears, dirty purple sneakers, and pens crowding her flannel breast pocket. No one else could ever look quite like her.

We went out to dinner seeking her new quest—the perfect calzone. Afterwards, we went to her favorite bookstore and bought photography books and some essays by Cynthia Ozick. Then we returned home and made extraordinary love, her vitality infectious. This morning she put on the record of *West Side Story* and we acted out the parts, singing and dancing around the living room before she left, clutching her carrot juice jar, to be a sociologist for a few hours. It is so replenishing when we play and dance. Eat new foods. When I bathe and oil her dry and flaking skin. Lie with her in bed and watch videotapes. To love in all the ways we love together. How lucky I am to have her.

Barbara
July 15

Time is like a long telephoto lens selecting something out of a wide range of vision and focusing in on it closely. Human perception of the future is like that too. We can never know the future in terms of a fully detailed, rich picture of ourselves, other people, and future situations. Rather, we take a present image and make it into a future moment and call it a goal or plan. And a goal is just as narrow as a telescopic lens selecting one sharp image out of a totally ambiguous future state of events.

But to live in a wide-angle, present day reality is to experience every day with incredible breadth, richness, and depth, feeling filled in every way. That is the way I live now. Each day is a dense chain of different kinds of beads, different kinds of experiences, threaded together by the continuity that is me. My emotions are always just one scratch below the surface. Each day is filled with a wide-ranging richness, from really deep laughter to inexpressible, inconsolable isolation. From connectedness with others to the beauty of perceiving the inner design and structure of all things.

Each day is filled with work, gardening, cooking, writing, music. I am filled with a sense of being here, being moved, being touched and both connected and alone in my life, my journey, my odyssey.

Blood Money

August – November 1985

Sandy

August 6

Barbara is nervous, preparing to give her mother and father more information about her diagnosis. They need to be prepared for the radiation, the length of time she will be on strong chemo, and still be left with a sense of optimism. A balancing act, but one that Barbara is determined to make. She sits on the window seat overlooking her garden, a yellow pad balanced on her knees, drafting all the possible directions the conversation might take.

Meeting with her cancer counselor yesterday, she was asked to describe a recent family crisis and the ways each member behaved. "That is how your family will respond this time," she was told. "Whatever their relationship to the crisis, their engagement or lack of it, their protectiveness or avoidance, it will be the same."

After she has written a likely scenario that includes their anticipated reactions, she calls me to the sofa where we rehearse the plan she has drawn up. Like a battle plan, all the pieces in place.

"What will you tell your mother when she asks why you didn't tell her everything when they were here?" I begin.

"I didn't want to worry her," she says firmly.

That is true. Barbara has never wanted to worry her parents and has kept many parts of her life from them. She has often criticized me for giving my mother what she felt was too much information. "Can't you see it will just upset her? What's the point of telling her something she can't understand and that will only aggravate her?" Good questions.

But for me the telling, however inappropriate it may have been, was always motivated by a desire to be known, to be seen by my mother. Visibility more important a consideration than protection. Barbara and I each had a relationship to "telling" that was quite different. And each equally unsuccessful.

Now, both of her parents are frail, in their mid-seventies; her mother has lymphatic cancer controlled successfully with chemotherapy, and her father is nearly blind and no longer able to work. Barbara can no longer protect them from information that will be "upsetting," "aggravating." Cancer has taken that protective option from her.

We drink tea and discuss ways to present the medical information, couch the words, make it palatable. As we plan, I find my thoughts drifting, trying to imagine receiving such a call from one of my own daughters.

How would they tell me if one of them had cancer? Would they tell each other first, as Barbara has done with her sister Ruth? My eldest daughter, Janaea, might have. She would first tell her partner, Tony, then her younger sister, Alison, and together with them face what needed to be done. She would protect me, I decide. She wouldn't want me to know until things were stable, doctors had been chosen, and treatment was already under way. Alison has no partner now, so I expect she would reach out toward me first. But if she had a partner—would she do the same? Might there be a time when I would become simply another psychological task to be managed in a time of crisis—with skill, tact, and love?

What would it feel like to know one of my daughters had cancer? What would be the "same" ways I would engage with them? What would they be able to predict from our decades together? Words, I suppose. Information, feelings, books. Talking. That's always been my answer to everything. But cancer doesn't respond to words.

I pull my attention back to what Barbara is saying. Force myself to remember the differences. Barbara's mother, Regina, barely escaped an emotionally impoverished childhood in Poland and lost nearly her entire family to the Nazis, leaving permanent scars of depression and terror at all the unforeseen dangers in the world.

David, her father, was rarely present because he worked six days a week, twelve hours a day to make a meager living for his family. Both parents, while expecting their daughters would become "workers," hoped they would go to college. They shifted all their dreams onto their children and immersed themselves relievedly in the new troubles, the little troubles, that made up their life in America.

Ruth lived too far away; Barbara had a boyfriend who was unsuitable. Barbara didn't eat well. Ruth was too thin and worked too hard. Barbara was anxious about tenure. No longer life-and-death matters as it had been for them growing up in Europe.

But now all that will change. Death and the struggle for life will enter their world again after so many decades of safety in America.

I feel disengaged and lonely as we talk. My mother, Barbara's parents, my daughters, Barbara's sister blur—a shifting series of images. The dreams I have for my children are the same as those of her parents. We share the sense of impotence at being unable to protect our children from the dangers that await them. Barbara's parents must now face the terrifying reality that their first-born may die before them. I grow fearful about losing my children. Losing Barbara. We are all in danger now.

Barbara

August 7

How do I disclose and to whom? Under what conditions does disclosure become relevant? Give it language, it becomes exposed to air. It breathes, it's alive: to tell is to make real. I must. I am impelled to reach out.

Disclosure begins as desperation, a frothing at the mouth, a constant foaming of anxiety. The anxiety is pervasive. So is my disclosure. Everyone has to know. I have no boundaries, no ability to differentiate among levels of friendship, levels of intimacy.

Later I can relax and allow enough time to elapse for me to observe and process other people's responses to me. I am able to differentiate and discriminate between friends. Some people have moved in closer. Others cannot bear to have lengthy conversations with me—they have disappeared. Others haven't visited. They haven't seen me bald or my head covered with my little cap.

Yet some, like Marinell and Stan, asked to look at my scar. Marinell even touched it.

Old lovers seem to have a harder time. T. didn't call for ten days after being told. J. has known for over a month and has not written. G. has known for at least two weeks, possibly three, and hasn't called. L. is upset and transparently ambivalent.

As I begin to observe them, I am able to classify types of response independent of previous intimacy. It's a new classification system with the heroes being "heart" people, those who can reach out, comfort, or write to share stories. People who can tolerate illness, sadness, and hardship are new friends. Those who have pulled back and not called—I don't mind. I'm not angry nor do I feel disappointed. I understand how it can be for them. Wasn't I afraid of June? Wasn't I afraid to be near her, seeing her death in front of me? Sandy is angry at them, thinking they have an obligation to overcome their own anxiety and behave with more decency. It's not that they are indecent. They are afraid.

Barbara

August 10

Today I was ecstatic, shot through with internal happiness. Even a sense of joy. Why? For the first time in a week I have energy instead of chemicals rushing through me. I can feel this energy pumping my heart and body. So much energy—three hours of intellectual energy, two hours of gardening energy. And music. Music. Singing along with Bernardo and Maria. Show tunes. Dancing with the ensemble in A *Chorus Line*. Washing that man right out of my hair.

My fingernails are dirty, chlorophyll-stained from gathering grass cuttings in the park. Four bags full for composting in my garden. Breaking up the clods, interspersing the cut grass, making the soil buoyant and light.

What extraordinary bodily pleasure to feel the stretches, tugs, and pulls in my muscles. The joy of being warm because I'm moving my body all the time. And the garden smells of earth and life. The music is loud as I shovel, dig, and get dirty. It's wonderful.

Naturally I did too much. My muscles hurt, my back aches, my shoulder is stiff from shoveling, but what pleasure! I love it—alive, alive, alive. Screaming alive. Fighting alive. Kicking alive!

Sandy

August 20

They have prepared Barbara's vulnerable chest to receive radiation, tracing a grid on it with a thick pen in geometric stains that enrage me. Pirate's treasure. "X" marks the spot. Dig it out. But her long throat and narrow shoulders seem familiar, the rest of her body remains fully fleshed and sturdy, and her hair is beginning to grow back.

This morning Barbara put on a dusty-rose blouse with puffed sleeves made of a silky fabric that rests gently upon her. Emerging from its neckline and extending towards her throat is a garish red line. Just as her relatives who survived the Nazi concentration camps had marked bodies, so I hope this too will be a mark of survival.

I look at a picture of her taken just one year ago during our holiday at Sea Ranch. She is naked, perched in front of a picture window, towel wrapped turbanlike around her head, smiling at the camera, at me. Her breasts and body are still intact. Our lives were still intact.

Yesterday as friends visited, Barbara sat in the window seat without her hat. Perhaps she is beginning to believe the many women who have told her that the shape of her head is lovely.

Sandy
August 25

Radiation began today.

Barbara
September 3

The side effects of radiation are extremely unpleasant, enervating, creeping in slowly and catching me unaware. I'm exhausted, but it's different from the exhaustion of chemotherapy. A different depletion, different sense of lassitude.

There is a terrible lump in my throat all the time. And it seems the only way to get rid of it is by swallowing. Yet swallowing is painful and hurts my throat even more. A cycle of pain and swallowing, swallowing and pain. My mouth is always full of saliva: the more I get nervous, the more I produce; the more I swallow, the more it hurts, the more I get nervous. All my throat muscles are in spasm, complicating whatever is going on in my esophagus.

My concentration is focused and deliberate. I need to get through radiation, with its fatigue and the terrible pain in my throat.

Barbara
September 8

The malpractice suit is looming in just a few weeks and my lawyer expects the arbitration to be tough. She needs to take many depositions and I have to hear details of the medical mistakes that were made that led to my shortened life. I will have to get a new CAT brain scan and have the old one reread.

I know there is a point, an important point to this fight. It's about women's bodies. It's a struggle to overcome negligence and incompetence. I try to remember.

Barbara
September 9

To have a cylindrical machine pointed at me, scanning me, is a terrifying experience, filling me with foreboding. The strain is unbearable. These machines with penetrating calibrating vision are the ultimate arbiters of truth. To engage with them is as emotion-laden as consulting the oracle.

Waiting is agony. Waiting for the machine to mechanically scan the body. Turn to the left. Move to the right. Don't move. Hold your breath. Relax. Undergoing the procedure feels like a form of torture I don't understand. Lying there stiffly, I weep.

When the procedure is completed, there is still the waiting time for interpretation. Are my lungs clear? Is there contamination in my bones? What about that pain in my elbow? My dizziness seems to be returning. It diminishes when I'm on chemotherapy but now I'm frightened that the cancer has metastasized to my brain. Is there evidence of more cancer?

I wait with Sandy, full of anxiety, heart beating hard and fast, until relief comes. "No, there's no cancer anywhere else that is currently detectable using this technology," the doctor says in the guarded language of diagnosis.

It's not enough, but it's all there is.

Barbara
September 11

The effects of radiation are terrible now and there is nonstop itching on the entire surface of my skin. I don't know who scratches more, my dog Sembei with her fleas or me with my burnt skin.

Sandy
September 12

I feel a pervasive sense of weariness. A heaviness presses against me, requiring more and more doggedness to lift, even for a few hours.

Each night I awake tantalized by rich, voluptuous images, phrases that shatter and disappear if I try to rise and write them down. This morning I went to my desk and saw scrawled in thick red pen, nearly the same color as the markings on Barbara's chest, the words, "I long—I long." I don't remember waking up, writing it down or, more importantly, what it was I longed for in the night. My appetites feel consuming, engulfing. Just below them lie the terror, the fear of abandonment, the roaring of grief and of muffled rage. How much acceptance of despair is a necessary part of the acceptance of living?

Barbara
September 13

Sandy is away again and I miss her very much. And I love her very much. I'm proud of the work we are doing together. Suffering is ordinary.

My parents have come back to San Francisco to be with me during the last ten days of radiation. They walk so cutely together, arms linked. My father steadies my mother—her arthritis makes walking difficult. She helps him see, his increasing blindness making navigating curbs and traffic harrowing. Their presence is wonderful. They make me feel good, peaceful, optimistic. My mother reassured me that the cancer won't come back and I believe her. A kind of belief, despite my knowing the statistics, the probabilities, the chances.

And now there are a dozen containers of homemade soup in the freezer.

Sandy
September 18

VANCOUVER. I have been working here for four days while Barbara's parents are at home with her. It seems hard for her to reach out to me, perhaps because her parents are there, perhaps because time has taken on such urgency. She talks now about having the house to herself more often, about writing, about wanting to travel with friends.

I admire and respect her tenaciousness and dignity in the face of this disease. Her loyalty to friends. Her protectiveness and love for her parents and sister. But my need to be central in her life feels overwhelming and I flounder in this new role. I feel isolated, lonely.

Barbara
September 18

When we are all together, I am relaxed, part of a system. But when first Sandy and then my parents left, I had tremendous separation anxiety. I felt like a seal or a baboon that's been separated from its mother. If I could, I would make those heartbreaking animal sounds that reach the deepest places of the soul to express my longing.

Barbara
September 20

Sandy is home now and we have begun to talk about preparing my legal and medical power of attorney. Clear talk, realistic, no bullshit. Anyhow, I've got a life to live, whatever its length.

Fall is in the air; the tomatoes are mature. Time for planting a winter garden. A quiet takes over. I must endure this radiation and following that, the arbitration, and following that, a year of chemotherapy. I will try to endure: with fortitude, with perseverance, with guts. With good cheer.

Sandy
September 28

We celebrated the end of radiation last week. The skin across her chest appears sunburned, red, and bubbly, and Barbara creams it every day with aloe. The image of her lying beneath the massive radiation machine, staring up at the ceiling while being zapped with poison, is permanently traced in my brain. Her indefatigable good spirits are as well.

The lawsuit is scheduled to begin soon and I am determined that "they" be held responsible for their shoddy medicine, their indifference. One doctor said in his deposition that he had met Barbara but he never did. Another lied about the wording of his report of the mammogram results. I will never forget the sound of his disembodied voice on our phone machine saying, "The mammo is clear but if you are still worried, go see a surgeon." He now insists he said,

"Be sure to see a surgeon"—which, of course, Barbara would have done. Their goddamn cavalier attitudes. The hasty examinations, inadequate information, and incorrect diagnosis. The way in which Barbara fell through the cracks of the system is intolerable to me.

But I know it's not just Barbara. Women should not be blamed, underserved, invisible, alone. Barbara isn't now, and no woman should ever be. Women have built movements before. We can do it again.

Sandy
September 30

Now I want to look ahead. To the end of chemo, radiation, lawsuits. To remission of whatever length. To a sort of dailiness that eludes us now. Everything is heightened, carries immediacy, feels portentous. Barbara and I went to Temple Sha'ar Zahav for *Yom Kippur*, the Day of Atonement, the most sacred of the Holy Days, and sobbed throughout the service. Both of us so raw, so unprotected. All our feelings on the surface now.

Barbara's bald head drew curious stares, many in our gay and lesbian congregation wondering if she had AIDS or cancer and was taking chemotherapy. Breast cancer strikes one in nine women now. The men and the women in this congregation, each with our own epidemic.

Now a business trip to Huntington and Little Rock, timed to coincide with Barbara's faculty meeting in Vermont. Our home empties as we ascend in planes taking us to different parts of the country. Barbara seems glad for the distraction of the meetings, the pleasure of a few old friends in Boston, the fall colors. She seems less anxious about the upcoming litigation and more thoughtful about the many and complex meanings of her upcoming tenure review.

Barbara
October 1

A fine spray coats the air, the trees are in half-silhouette against the strange lightness of this fog, punctuated by a yellow accent of an autumn leaf that pierces through the mist, as I write in my journal before a faculty meeting.

There are seven dead flies on the floor, this room is airless and stale, my nose is stuffy and I have a million feelings simmering beneath the surface. I'm lonely and sad on this balmy night. I wish Sandy were here. I miss her soothing body next to mine, and the comfort of Sembei in the next room. I miss my garden and my home. I miss my mother and father and feel panicky that I have not been able to reach them on the phone. I'm very weepy and melancholy about my limitations.

All my life I wanted to be a tenured university professor. I had the outsider's romantic vision of tweed jackets, heather sweaters, blazing sunsets. A fireplace with a good book and music afterwards. Tenure. The stamp of legitimacy. The guarantee of lifetime employment and a pension for retirement.

I went up for tenure once and was so shattered by the process and its outcome that I did a 180 degree turn and took an academic job in a nontraditional program that eschewed the entire system. But now they too have instituted tenure, after all that ideological idealism.

Tenure is a ranked system of statuses, a hierarchy of offices through which one moves. It begins in graduate school, which is oversupplied with excellent people, many of whom, for one reason or another, cannot or will not make it in academia. Candidates are continuously weeded out. Some get prized fellowships. Others get prime jobs in universities. Most don't.

The neophyte teaches, writes, publishes, gets grants, makes connections, becomes visible, and learns the politics of being properly mentored in a department. For females, having an older male advocate is still traditional, like the father giving away the bride. The same is true for men, who have always performed this function for each other.

Tenure is a peculiar form of social organization that mixes aspects of mobility with those of kinship. The young ones of the tribe fiercely compete for the prize, for who will be one of the next generation's carriers of knowledge. They are evaluated on the basis of three factors—magnitude, velocity, and quality. The amount one publishes is not enough. It must be evaluated in terms of the trajectory of time. And quality, too, that elusive ingredient.

The initiation process consists of a series of tests the candidate has to pass. As in most initiations, she must show courage and strength, especially in such ceremonial rituals as prelims, orals, and job searches. In a system that emphasizes criticism, attack, and counterattack, the neophyte must learn to defend herself against competition-induced behaviors like one upmanship. Because it is based on a zero-sum game, where one's status is diminished by someone else's good performance, the candidate must show decorum and cool where others might get rattled, upset, argumentative, or lose control. The ethos of "good work" runs concurrently with the norms of "good performance." Not only should one's work be empirically sound, theoretically sophisticated, and tightly reasoned, it helps enormously if the presentation is witty, clever, entertaining, written with such rhetorical devices as an in joke or an elegant turn of phrase. Camouflaged and cloistered in the niceties of genteel discourse, the academic attack and counterattack argument can be just as vicious as tribal warfare. In an ongoing series of battles, the initiate shows elders and peers that she is made of the right stuff—that she can survive in their world.

Then after a seven-year trial period, the elders make their judgment. Those who succeed are given a permanent place and the rules that previously defined their efforts are no longer applicable. Instead, one's rights and obligations change. There are new roles: that of the media spokesperson, the grant entrepreneur, the administrative head. There are new rules, rules of kinship and belonging, a sense of community, and responsibility to fairly share the tasks that must be performed by these elders.

This year, the same year as my diagnosis, the same year I learned I have five years left to live, I will be given tenure. I will die knowing I have arrived, obtained peer and elder approval—knowing I am made of the right stuff. A bittersweet lifetime guarantee.

Barbara
October 8

I feel crazed! At 8 a.m. yesterday, an ordinary morning, I was out at a construction site gathering irregularly shaped blocks of scrap wood for the fireplace in my office.

Just three and a half hours later everything was changed. I was sitting in my lawyer's office listening to the phone call which radically changed my post-diagnosis life. Kaiser settled my case before trial for $296,000 plus $25,000 a year, increasing 3 percent annually for the length of my life. Which makes me very rich.

Barbara
October 25

This is the most discombobulating thing that has ever happened to me. When I got the diagnosis, my first impulse was to reach out to people. To be close. To connect with people I loved. Now there are secrets. I am advised not to tell anyone. Not to talk about the dollar amount. I feel pressures to support this organization or that family member. There are gifts I want to give.

The most unsettling thing about all of this is that I'm a person who rarely has had fantasies. Now I feel so ungrounded and have spending fantasies every other minute. Travel, research assistants, books, art work, gifts to my family, investments. Even more so because the money from Kaiser is just for me. Between Kaiser and Vermont College's insurance, most of my medical bills will be paid for separately.

I've been on tranquilizers to try to calm down. Ordinary life— going to the office, reading—helps to quiet this ongoing panicky feeling.

Sandy
October 26

It's been just a few weeks since Barbara's settlement and my feelings fill me with anxiety and confusion. My hand feels heavy as I write. A price tag on Barbara's life.

I walk on the university campus in South Dakota, and the barren trees, the feel of the air on my skin, evoke the bleak landscape of New England after the leaves have fallen, the ground hard and closed. Everything poised for the first snow. And I feel like the girl I once was, walking home from elementary school, little and lonesome, waiting for winter.

When I was that child, all "naughtiness" was punished in the same way. My allowance was cut off. All good grades or good behavior was rewarded with a present. Money was the currency of emotions.

I have never accumulated money and always gave it away when I had even a bit more than I needed. Now Barbara wants to spend this new money on herself. On her family. On me. But for me to have money means I am no longer myself. I will become my mother. A woman with money.

My father, during his final years, felt like a failure about not having accumulated "enough" money and was (perhaps like his own father) unable to see and enjoy what he had. Money was always the arbiter of success for him.

Somehow all this makes me feel I was robbed. Betrayed by Barbara's cancer. Unable to identify the thief—wondering if something was my fault. If I was bad or undeserving. Not destined for the riches I really wanted. Having money instead.

And then there's my confusion about all this money. Is it ours? Hers? Do I want to be consulted about its distribution? What would it feel like to be supported? Part of me yearns to be taken care of in that way, but even my mother cautions me not to lose my life in Barbara's, much as she was lost in my father's. I haven't been a wife in over twenty-five years but can imagine myself having time to fix fresh flowers for the table, prepare nourishing meals, take long walks, travel together. I want to come to rest alongside Barbara now—to make a nest for us, sit quietly in our yard, cherishing her and the time we have left. Such dependency frightens me even as I long for it.

Sandy
October 30

Last night I wrote, "I am excused. I excuse myself. Cancer is what I do now." Cancer is my work. Barbara's mood swings, doctor's appointments, medicines. My feelings. Our writing together. All of it has become my central activity. Cancer swallows up the air of my life and insinuates its presence everywhere. Nothing remains untouched. Inviolate.

So I am excused. I don't want to be separate now. Time is too valuable. I will be separate soon enough. I am excused. I excuse myself from autonomy. I need now to yield, to allow the dependence on this woman who has become my life.

Barbara
October 30

With all this focus on the medical malpractice suit and financial settlement, I have lost a quiet center. There are too many people in my life now. Doctors, lawyers, financial advisers. It's time to get back to quiet. To read, write book reviews, work with students, go to the opera. Time to think. It is so noisy and quivery inside me.

The ironies of blood money are deeper than I ever imagined. No one would trade money for what I have to go through. Money is nothing. I never wanted it. If I had wanted money, I would have worked for it in some business or corporation. I would have learned money management and public relations skills, like how to build motivation or morale. At least, I would have learned bookkeeping.

No. I wanted time. Time to read and to think, to walk my dog. (I thought at one time, to have a child.) Time to contemplate the intense orange of a persimmon. Time to take pictures. To argue with other thinkers. To cut wood for the fireplace.

I don't have so much time anymore. The horizon line of my life comes in closer and closer. A day is so precious. I want to cram everything into it.

That's the way the system works. Redress for grievances. But in my soul, my heart, it rings horribly of a Faustian pact with the devil.

This money in exchange for years of my life. $1,000 for every vomit. $1,000 for every cut, every needle in my arm. Every gag. Every wave of nausea. Every hurt, pain, and ache in my body. Every nosebleed. Every anguished moment. No sane person would make such a contract.

Sandy
November 4

Barbara's mother fell and is in the hospital with a broken hip. Her father, blind and diabetic, is unable to give himself his necessary daily insulin shots because he cannot see which vial is empty and which is full. Their dependency on each other. My dependency on Barbara.

Barbara
November 5

NEW YORK. Last week, my mother fell, broke her hip, was hospitalized and is now having physical therapy. No one called me for days. My father didn't tell me when we spoke on the phone; my sister left messages to call but never said why. I'm angry at everyone but, most of all, I feel like a nine-year-old child again. This is the worst, hardest to deal with, not being included. Being lied to.

And I see, sadly, that I recapitulated the lying they did to me— the secret of my mother's depression and electroshock therapy when I was nine—when I kept the seriousness of my cancer from them. All in the stupid name of protection from hurt, sparing the other, not understanding that the despair of exclusion and isolation is far more of a burden than the truth.

I have a much deeper understanding of family secrets and I am very sad. I also feel incredibly helpless, imagining my mother's pain. I have never felt so close and bonded to her as in these last months, since I told her I have cancer. With the telling came the closeness. A closeness that has been sitting inside of me, burning for forty years. I feel so tied to her, so corded, so umbilically connected.

Barbara
November 9

I feel numb. My father is in the hospital now with a mild heart attack; my mother hobbling around on a walker. And I am here in Brooklyn, between the second and third round of chemotherapy cycles, to help them. Still and always the oldest daughter.

I make daily trips to Coney Island Hospital, talk to the doctors, take my mother to the surgeon, and all the while, try to remain cheerful and cope with everything. That's all I do, it seems. Cope.

I have displaced affect this week—the kind where I cry at television sentimentality or stare in awe at a photograph on a book about Yosemite, but see my own mother's face as ordinary.

Yesterday I watched my father sleeping and imagined he was dead and I was at his funeral. His face, flaccid, looked so different. It made me aware of his aliveness, his animation, his life force present in his constantly changing and expressive face. Later I looked at my mother sleeping. She seems peaceful, the medical report good. Her prognosis is excellent and she's ready for a quad cane. Today was long and difficult, her first day out in weeks, but she did wonderfully. She even dressed up for the occasion!

My heart breaks at the thought of leaving them to return home. Separation anxiety. Guilt. It weighs me down, so much that I can barely imagine being light enough to fly. Just to be able to cope. To handle everything.

In My Own Time

Barbara

Watching someone else spend their last months on earth can be a mirror for clarifying one's own choices. I was fortunate to have this experience in a compressed form: I watched a film about someone dying. That someone was Barbara Myerhoff and the evening became a turning point in my life.

I had a lot of anticipatory ambivalence about this film. Barbara Myerhoff was a well-known anthropologist, who just before her illness was chair of the Anthropology Department at the University of Southern California. She had written *Number Our Days*, a book about Jewish senior citizens living in an old-age center in Venice. With Lynn Littman, she had adapted the book into a film that won an Academy Award for the best documentary of 1977. As a young scholar, she had done her fieldwork among Indians, studying the process of achieving ecstasy through the peyote ritual. In fact, ritual was her strongest interest and she passionately wanted to understand how people used rituals in their lives to create meaning and to surrender to ecstasy. As a mature anthropologist, she was still fascinated by the same themes that had compelled her earlier.

Just before her diagnosis she was studying the lives of Chassidic Jews, some of whom were American-born and had found Orthodoxy after a period of "normal" growing up, and others of whom were brought up within the tradition. These disparate strands then found each other and made community. Myerhoff wanted to understand the phenomenon she called a "voluntary ghetto."

Because of the critical and financial success of their first documentary, Lynn Littman agreed to collaborate on another. However, in June of 1984, during the early stages of that project, Barbara was diagnosed with mesothelioma, the kind of cancer that is usually associated with exposure to asbestos. She was given only six months to live, which turned out to be accurate. She died in January, 1985. Because of her cancer, the film's central focus changed. Now called *In Her Own Time*, it became the story of how Barbara faced her death through the lens of her anthropological exploration of Orthodox Judaism.

Because she was an academic celebrity, I knew about her work. I also knew she was a consultant to the Traveling Jewish Theater, a group that shared her interest in ritual and its application in drama. We knew some of the same people. And we knew friends of friends who sooner or later would have introduced us. But she died before we ever met. She was a person I would have wanted to know.

I entered the Palace of Fine Arts in San Francisco filled with intensely strong, often conflicting feelings, and perhaps deeper expectations. I was turning to her, to this film, to help me find a way through my own cancer.

I knew that someday I would face the issues that Barbara Myerhoff would face in this film. Perhaps she could show me a path I could adopt as my own. After all, she was an academic—I'm an academic. She was Jewish—I am Jewish. She was an intellectual—I'm an intellectual. I thought I could learn something about what lay before me, find that her way of approaching the living-before-dying period could be my way too. I did learn something from the movie, but not what I had expected: it would be my own path, not the other Barbara's.

The movie began and we saw Barbara Myerhoff walking along Fairfax Avenue, the Jewish section of Los Angeles, describing the history of the neighborhood, the people, and the area. Like all good social scientists, she mixes some objective description with the emotional impact the facts have on people's lives. She tells us that even though she is Jewish, entering this community she feels foreign: "I feel as if I walked in a New Guinean village in my own backyard."

She sits with a woman whose work is to fit traditional Orthodox wives for *sheitels*, wigs to cover their close-cropped hair. Tradition requires that a woman reveal her hair only to her husband. Barbara, too, was trying on wigs, knowing she would need one after chemotherapy when her hair fell out.

In another scene, Barbara tells an Orthodox rabbi who has befriended her that she has cancer. Together they write a letter to a famous Lubavitch rabbi in Israel to ask for his guidance. She begins, "I am a professor of anthropology. In June, I learned that I have lung cancer. I've had two courses of chemotherapy which have not been successful. Now it appears that there are no medical actions which are helpful. I am now looking at Judaism much more seriously. I am looking for a miracle."

In the film a ritual will be performed that is rarely done in Judaism and hardly ever done for women. Barbara will be given a new name so that the angel of death, when it comes looking for her, will be tricked and will not find her. This requires that Barbara engage in a cleansing ritual—the *mikvah* bath—before she can be renamed. In Judaism, practically everything—including all the laws, the habits, the customs, the prescribed behaviors—centers on the concept of holiness. A state of great purity allows your wishes to come true. In order to enter the "holy," Barbara must be clean from top to bottom. The area underneath her fingernails must be scraped; her hair must be washed: every strand must be clean. She must stand in the tub, spread her legs, and squat energetically down into the water so that the water is forced up into her vaginal canal. That, too, must be clean. She must take the mucous out of her eyes, wash her nose, take the wax out of her ears, make sure every spot on and in her body is ready to enter holiness. Barbara is instructed in the details of *mikvah* by the rabbi's wife and, after each of three total immersions in the bath, the rabbi's wife pronounces Barbara "kosher."

While Barbara was performing the *mikvah* ritual bath, she spoke to us, the audience, like an anthropologist in a travelogue narrating an exotic adventure. She conveyed the temperature of the water ("just like body temperature"), how it felt to be immersed in such a way ("it's something I can see doing again"). Although she said she was looking for a miracle, and I believed the solemnity of that declaration, she did not seem to be "in it." She was merely doing it. She describes the ritual as a "membrane" and says, "I can see through it, but I can't walk through it."

The only exception is when Barbara obtains a *get* (a Jewish divorce). The rabbi advises her that she needs her *neshoma* (soul) back before she can die and the only way is by divorcing her ex-husband in an Orthodox ceremony. It was a stirring sequence and the ceremony of divorce was the only place where I felt her fully engaged and present.

We see the men gathered in the *shul* as Barbara sits alone. In Orthodox synagogues, men and women are spatially segregated into different seating areas. The men are *davening*, moving their bodies back and forth rhythmically as their voices cry out in prayer. In a very rare, solemn, and profound moment, Barbara is given a new name— Channah Batia Feige—and, with tentative, wistful conviction, tells us, the audience, that she hopes this is her miracle.

But always, I felt her professional identity at the center of this story. You could see her agile mind at work, see the wheels brilliantly turning, could sense the electricity of her mind. But what I didn't see was a fifty-year-old woman facing the realities of her illness, telling us how she felt about her life. What I didn't see was a woman facing the ending of her life clearly and consciously, without defense and without denial. She seemed to be using her work identity as a protection against her forthcoming death.

I felt like I was the only person in the audience who thought the film was a celebration of Barbara's denial of her impending death. I certainly felt alienated from those who seemed to respond to her fierce determination to work until the very end of her life. I thought they didn't see how profoundly defended against her feelings she was. Didn't she want to know anything about herself or work on unresolved issues in her life? All she seemed to want to do was her damned study until the day she died.

I quickly understood that I was going to choose a different path. Instead of looking away, I wanted to experience everything. I wanted to savor every feeling, every emotion, every wave of sensation and thought that would originate inside of me. I wanted to develop all those aspects of myself that were only partly alive, that still yearned for a voice, for visibility, so that they could see the light of day and then become integrated into a larger sense of self. I wanted to sing and dance and play music and travel. There was so much I hadn't done. I didn't want to die without experiencing many, many more things. I was already a sociologist. I didn't want to die doing another study.

The major identity change I made was my decision to be public with my cancer. I was going to enter it, use it, embrace it, and eventually incorporate it as part of me. I was going to write about it in my journals, in my articles. I was going to counsel women who needed help. My doctor asked me if I'd be willing to talk to newly diagnosed patients, telling them something about my experience with the drugs, with the hairlessness, with the vomiting. I had already been doing this for a while with friends of friends who had been diagnosed. My name had become affiliated with two support groups and I was already handling a number of calls. Sandy and I wrote a piece, which would be expanded to become this book, and it was published in *Sinister Wisdom*, a lesbian literary magazine.

Our first collaboration, "Reverberations" [appearing here as the first chapter, "Coming Home"], had been written years before and published in *The Tribe of Dina: A Jewish Women's Anthology*. It was a reflection on the ways Sandy and I are different kinds of Jews and we had read excerpts together at a series of women's bookstores. At each reading I learned that the words felt different in my mouth each time, that they had new meanings, new flavors, that they were not fixed, nor did they come out as I intended when I wrote them. I learned the power of the spoken word. Up until then I only had known about the power of the printed word.

I began to write in a new style. Instead of using sociological data as the basic scaffolding upon which to build an interpretation, I found there were many things I could write about simply because I was human and articulate. I no longer needed "the data" to tell the story. I went inside myself and wrote about my life and my feelings.

My world widened and stretched, allowing new interests to develop and transform themselves into other interests. I had always been that kind of a learner, someone who had roamed freely through ideas, someone who followed the footnotes, wherever they led. It seemed like I ended up very far away from the original question, but when I looked back over the quest, I saw that I had not travelled far from the original impulse at all, but took a winding path, a spiral perhaps, that always deepened the journey.

Learning new things is the most intense way that I know I'm alive. I'm always standing at the edge of some new interest. In fact, I would even coin a phrase for myself: a neophile. Someone who loves new things. New tastes, new sounds, new ideas. I get intellectually restless very easily.

Once, when I was a teenager listening to the radio late at night, a disc jockey talked about Charlie Parker, the great jazz alto saxophone player. He described how Charlie Parker would go to Hungarian nightclubs and Jewish weddings to absorb a wide range of ethnic music so that he could expand his understanding of harmony. So from my earliest exposure to jazz, I started listening to Hungarian music, just to hear, just to imagine for one earthly second, what Hungarian music may have sounded like to a Black jazz musician. But then I discovered that I liked the sound of it myself, which put me on a path that led to the folk harmonies of Bulgaria, which led to Bartok, which led to Kodaly, which led to orchestration, which led to Ravel, which led to underlying classical structure, which led to Bach—which brought me back to jazz.

Through these intellectual and aesthetic journeys, I've learned that there are structures that tie together the threads of my seemingly disparate tastes. My world appears to be composed of microbe-like trails of inquiry, scatterings and skitterings, stochastic models, mathematical improbabilities. Sometimes when I look through my life as if I'm looking through a microscope, I see long lines, like bacterial chains, not necessarily intersecting, but co-existing. Each line is a path I've followed, each line a compelling adventure, each line representing an interest I've followed. They are autonomous, self-generated, self-seeking, self-limited paths of intense intellectual curiosity.

During this year off, I have remembered who I am and, more importantly, what it means to be alive. Like Barbara Myerhoff, I have my *neshoma*—my soul—back and I have remembered how it feels to have each part in its proper place, each part fitting into a whole. Like Barbara Myerhoff, I have come back to my work, my writing, as the most important part of my life. I understand now, as I didn't when I first saw the film, that work doesn't have to be an intellectual defense against feeling one's emotions. It can simply be what a person loves to do. I now believe Barbara Myerhoff found herself, immersed herself, in those experiences and, finally, I understand and empathize much more with her choices.

I've come to understand that each of us must choose our own way of spending that time of living-before-dying. I no longer need to be so judgmental about the path she chose. We are each responsible for—and to—the time we have left. We each must consciously choose how to spend that time so that it doesn't evaporate into meaninglessness.

I have spent my time living a life that is committed to nondenial, experiencing all that I can experience in order to be fully aware. To live and to die consciously is what I want. This means being a vessel, porous and transparent, letting the emotions rise and fall, letting heartbreak come and letting it go, feeling the emotional pain, keeping it all moving, not blocked. It means opening myself to the rapid oscillation or rapid processing of discontinuous feelings, going from states of intense joy and pleasure to deep sadness and loss, to rage and anger, to peacefulness and then back to agitation and anxiety. It means living all the emotions, all the feelings. Letting them come and go. Not blocking them. There may be a physical tumor in me, one location where all the cells congregate, but I am working very hard to make sure there isn't an emotional tumor in me, a mass that has the power to block the flow of feelings. I have cancer but it is not consuming me. Rather, I am as alive as I can be; my creative juices have never been as electric; my thoughts have never been as clear. With each new status in my illness, my range of choices shrinks but I become deeper and richer, clearer and simpler to myself.

LIFE BENEATH THE SURFACE

DECEMBER 1985 – JUNE 1986

Barbara
December 6

Sandy and I are flying to Australia. I doze, and awaken, my thoughts returning to the past year, the altered time that began on February 22, 1985, each day crystal sharp and etched with precision in my mind. I remember those glorious weeks Sandy and I had at Sea Ranch during the summer of 1984. The last vacation before the diagnosis. When we still thought we would grow old together.

I put the earphones on to shift my attention and I listen first to Purcell's *Te Deum*, then a wonderful woodwind piece by Gounod called *Petite Symphonie in B-flat for Wind Instruments*.

As the plane circles for landing, I begin to grow excited about everything that awaits us here. So far I'm okay. My eyes feel greasy and teary, without lashes. My skin hurts. My urethra burns when I urinate. My nose still bleeds. But I am alive and kicking and enthusiastic. That's what counts.

Barbara
December 8

If I were to say this island is paradise, it would be a cliché, but it's an accurate description. The food is impeccable, gourmet dining at every meal. The water is the right temperature for swimming at either 6 a.m. or 6 p.m. It is the clearest, least muddy water I have ever seen in my life. Snorkeling is absolutely astonishing and not as difficult as I thought.

The other guests are another tribe entirely—the international rich—Australian families with unbelievably well-mannered children, Italian couples covered with gold, a German transvestite diver, American corporate executives with sullen and strained wives. A heterogeneous tribe, worthy of minute inspection as any good disciple of Mead, Benedict, and Malinowski might attest.

Sandy's need to intellectualize about class betrays an underlying uneasiness and lack of comfort with these surroundings. I, on the other hand, feel completely entitled and not at all interested in making astute observations. Indeed, I'm hardly making conversation, so inwardly content and unanxious am I. Perhaps I am dull company for Sandy. This is a new aspect of myself—totally unanxious.

Sandy
December 8

It was a grueling beginning for both of us: preparing to leave, packing, Barbara's fear about being so far away from her doctors. I was afraid of being drained and exhausted by her insistence on seeing every botanical garden and zoo. But after a not-so-bad, seventeen-hour flight, we find ourselves in the most magnificent tropical island I could ever have imagined. Only forty-four guests and thirty in staff. Exquisite and sumptuous meals. Coral reefs. Tropical vegetation.

I feel an unexpected and surprising shyness, tallness, awkwardness with these affluent white Christians. This place evokes very adolescent memories of being "other." Barbara too seems shy, stays close to me—watches.

Barbara
December 10

Yesterday morning at five-thirty we hiked as the sun moved higher into the sky. It was hard—the humidity of the tropics causes me to sweat profusely. Sandy, wearing only a bathing suit, seemed to fare better than I. We came upon a short path that led to the most pristine, isolated, secluded beach I have ever seen. Since I had a shirt and short pants on, and didn't want them to get wet, I took my clothes off and went swimming naked.

Freedom, complete freedom for my mutilated body. Freedom to swim, to move, to announce to the world I am whole in spirit if not in form, with an inkling of wholeness in my new form. Sandy and I snuggled in the water, her body unbelievably comforting and close to mine. Glorious freedom painted on her face as well.

Later in the day Sandy and I went to Mermaid Cove to snorkel. There is a great, cavernous life just under the surface. We wear our swim suits all day and my body feels so good. So alive. Whole again. Strong again. Normal again. Yet my hair is quite short and I see how much I have aged this year. I hardly recognize myself now when I look in the mirror. A middle-aged woman, fatter face and all. No one knows I wear a false breast in my bathing suit. When I came out of the water today, I unthinkingly squeezed my foam rubber tit; its sponginess accumulates water. Private joke on the world—or on me.

Sandy
December 10

Almost as soon as we arrived, when I eased into the green water for the first time, I felt the mantle of responsibility slip away, its weight slough off my skin and drift out to sea. I sleep long and deeply here and already have some color in my face. Barbara and I have just returned from a splendid adventure on our own dinghy, packed with a picnic lunch and snorkeling equipment as we toured this Sybaritic island.

It is a stunning and quieting experience to drift under the water alongside the coral and fish. The textures are unbelievable—spiky, rubbery, soft. Clams with deep openings filled with shiny, porous flesh. Schools of fish of all colors swimming in the utter stillness of their environment. I try to move with grace and stealth so as not to disturb them, floating on the clear exterior of the water as I witness what is just inches below: brain coral, staghorn, blue starfish. Hovering on the water, looking down into the life beneath the surface seems to parallel my careful observations of those I love, trying to see just under the veneer of their faces into their psyche, their unconscious, their underworld. How rich, variegated and full of colors we are, like these coral, these fish. A new world opening itself slowly to me.

Sandy
December 12

We found a secluded beach after breakfast where we swam naked, taking joy in our bodies, the clear water, and each other. We snorkeled, holding hands as we moved under the water, pointing out fish, turning our masked faces, imagining each other's smile.

It's now late afternoon. I have just returned from a swim and Barbara is still asleep. When she awakens, it will be time for her to begin chemotherapy again. She will take twenty-eight methotrexate and three cytoxan tablets. I feel enraged and very protective of her. She wanted so little in her life and worked so hard to achieve it. But much of it eluded her. Marriage, children, tenure, intellectual success. But I remember too that because of those failures, I became both her true love and the compromise of her middle years.

Barbara
December 17

New Zealand. We arrived in Auckland late this afternoon and I slept fitfully with a terrible dream. I was in an old-age home and wanted to escape, except they wanted to drug me. If I resisted the drugs it meant lockup. In the dream it was constructed as a catch-22. But when I looked at the injections, they were filled with tubes of red fluid—Adriamycin. I woke up thinking (as I have all along on this trip) that there is no escape from this cancer. But there are times my attention isn't on it, like when I'm snorkeling or operating a boat or writing or worrying about driving on the other side of the road.

I feel safe and secure with Sandy. There is no place I'd rather be than at Sandy's side, no matter where I am, any place in the world. Our chemistry is magic.

Barbara
December 19

Yesterday we saw caves lit with hundreds and thousands of glow-worms, had a wonderful dinner of lamb and fine claret, bought cotton camisoles. We are in Invercargill, the closest land mass to the Antarctic. It doesn't get dark until 10:30 p.m. and the sun rises at 5:30 a.m. I am photographing like crazy; the light is dazzling.

Today we drove to Milford Sound, fjords everywhere, waterfalls creating themselves from teeming rain. It is so moist in the world. Sheep and lambs are also everywhere in the rolling hills of the New Zealand countryside. We stop the car to watch them and try to talk to them but they are not social with humans, like dogs are. They are afraid of us and stick to themselves. They are right to be afraid and that knowledge touches my heart.

Sandy
December 20

I puzzle about the skills I've developed. I know such a great deal about the world of people, their nuances and interactions, and so little about the natural world. But that is the part of this trip I so love. The more secluded we are, the fewer people with whom we have to interact; the more untouched the countryside, the happier I feel. And yet I am so unfamiliar with the lives of trees, water, wildflowers, and animals that I feel like a trespasser in a way I rarely do in the city. Here I am an onlooker, an outsider longing for a way to apprehend the relationships of living things.

I sit now, looking out of the window in Milford Sound, facing massive fjords piercing the cloud cover, rushing waterfalls coursing over the rocks, seals idling on the wet crevices. The room is still,

Barbara asleep on the bed behind me, and I look out at a landscape as unfamiliar as the underwater world of coral and fish we have just left.

Barbara
December 23

It is a chemo day. I cried when I took the methotrexate tablets. Already my nose has begun to bleed. My fingernails are turning discolored, ridges disappearing.

Sandy
December 23

Fjords, caves with rushing waterfalls and glowworms clinging to the ceiling lighting our way. Snorkeling, drives through rolling fields where the sheep resemble silvery minnows moving slowly through a green sea, thousands of them, placid and doomed.

Now we return to the hotel where Barbara counts out twenty-eight yellow pills and begins to weep. Helplessly I put my hand on her back, making awkward circles with my palm as she puts one, then another, faster now, in groups of two or three, into her mouth, until they are all consumed. We stand beside each other wordlessly as Barbara drains the water glass, then turns to me, announcing brusquely, "Let's go for a walk. I need to move. I can't stay in this room now." I rise, splash cold water on my face, place an arm around her thickening waist and lead her outside. In two days we'll return home.

Sandy
February 22

Barbara and I planned a rebirth party to celebrate the first year since the day of diagnosis. Our friends came, with gifts and love. Barbara, who had only occasional birthday parties as a child, was subdued but pleased with the "fuss." There was champagne, stories, delight in her presence.

I remain watchful, a bit outside, feeling lost in the midst of the attention Barbara is receiving. I prepare, create, orchestrate these moments, but cannot always locate myself within them. After the presents are opened, the ribbons strewn at Barbara's feet, Marinell quietly gives me a card, the only one I receive. As I read its simple and loving message my eyes fill, "For Sandy, who has been there all year." Now she and David are moving to Santa Fe and I feel very alone.

My thoughts return to my father's death, just five years ago. I remember how similarly divided I felt. The adult, competent, resourceful part of me attended to the funeral details, to my mother's needs, to the financial affairs. But the other part of me was unnoticed, lost, and frightened. She was the child who thought her daddy was a giant. A man whose head touched the sky. The man who taught her to ice skate, play the piano, eat lobsters. The man whose car she listened for in the late afternoon when she was supposed to be doing her homework. The man who was the most handsome, unlike all the ugly boys in school. The man she was sure she would marry when she got big. That self found my father's death incomprehensible. For my daddy was larger than life and such a man cannot possibly die.

Now I imagine myself without Barbara, the woman I was to grow old with. The woman I did marry when I got big. The woman who taught me to play and to take my mind seriously. Barbara was my genesis, the spark of my unfolding. Will I shrink back to who I was when we met? Does my life require her presence? I am afraid of closing up, becoming brittle and lonely again.

Barbara
April 9

VERMONT ON MY FORTY-THIRD BIRTHDAY. Here in Vermont, I miss my house and Sandy, our routine, the dog, the talk shows I watch on Sunday, the garden. I want quiet, but quiet with Sandy. Intimate quiet. The conviviality of colleagues and a dormitory life are nice for forty-eight hours. After that the gnawing need for Sandy arises in me.

I read a lot, talk with friends, settle things that matter. Create a peaceful world so I can eventually leave it clearly and calmly. I did some of that with my brother-in-law Marc. Some with Ruth as well.

A bit with my colleagues. There is so much to do. I feel great relief at the prospect of not working for a year. But oh God, how afraid I am of an early recurrence.

During these past months, I have been struggling internally with the pressure to do something "significant." My work identity runs through my very cellular structure. For me, work is like a religion. I have devoted my life to it. Being a sociologist has been central to my identity and now I am giving that up. I was frightened when I thought of going on disability. Would they write "disabled professor" on my records at the hospital? I have never stopped working before, except for occasional summer vacations. I have never had a sabbatical, never consciously entered a period in which I decided to abandon previous habits and interests and just "wait and see" how I'd be. Will I be productive? Will I piss away the time? Can I keep writing? And will I write? Will I stay in bed and be depressed because I have cancer and no one knows how long I have to live? What am I going to do with a whole year?

It comes with the territory, I suppose, a pressure to do the "last hurrah" piece of work: something meaningful, something brilliant, something that will cause people to say, "Isn't it a shame she died so young—and so talented." There are many possibilities. One is to take the time to complete my unfinished work. I have stacks of academic papers that need revising, new writing, more references, better arguments. Since nothing hangs over my head like incomplete work, I feel an internal nagging to complete these papers. But do I actually want to spend months of my life revising old first and second drafts? Hardly! I haven't the time to spend on transforming youthful, clever insights into grown-up contributions to the literature.

My mind was my union card and has always been extraordinarily central to my life. I think of it as the place where I make my money. I work with my mind. I labor with my mind. My curiosity is part of my vitality; it's brought me pleasure and is a central way I see myself. I escaped many fates by having a good mind.

Peter used to tease me, when I told him I wanted to open a flower shop after college, that I never would. I would go to school and get a Ph.D. in horticulture instead. He was right about me.

All my life I just woke up each morning and began to work. But now the scales have shifted. If before I could have described myself as more mind-body, it's now body-mind. My mind is still very important to me, but it's not a source of great pleasure right now. It's just keeping me intact. My mind is so engaged with day-to-day that I can hardly think about anything else. It's not soaring. It's not free. It's hinged to my body. I'm usually a very productive person. But now it's like I have a second job. Having a disease and learning about it is literally patient work.

The book I most seriously considered writing in the past year was to be on medical malpractice. I outlined it, structured its organization carefully, and came up with reasonable and plausible notions about the transformation of medical relationships in American life: the decline of trust, the diminishing number of family doctors, the rise of specialization, the infiltration of contractual rights and obligations in a nonadversarial relationship that had previously been essentially paternalistic. Good ideas, yet it seems like another smart, focused, narrow project whose results I could imagine even before I started.

In a free-associative fantasy, I came up with an idea for a different sort of book. A photo-essay about women with breast cancer. It would bring together the best of who I am — photographer, thinker, feeler, interviewer — into a single meaningful strand.

I want to do work now that is moving and stirring, not merely smart and academically well reasoned. I want to touch on life's cruel ironies, on the bigger questions of courage, humanity, the meaning of time, the experience of bodily disintegrity, and the struggle to become whole to oneself.

Sandy

April 12

Last night a quiet bath helped me contain the maelstrom of emotions the day had created in me. Barbara's style is so unlike mine. More spare, less excessive, lean and focused. (Her first gift to me, a small red doorknob.)

We spoke for a long time tonight about Barbara's struggle to be "meaningful" with her time, her money, her work. She is worried about her nephew, Asher, and her responsibility to him. How big a gift should she give him? A bond, I suggest. A bond for college. Unstated is our knowledge that she will never see him enter college. She wants to please her sister, do the right thing, but is resentful about leaving money in place of herself.

I am more able now to acknowledge some of the ways I collude with Barbara to be larger than her own sized life—so that she as my partner will mirror my identity as someone often seen as larger than life. I worry that her choices will be offerings to please me. I cannot allow myself to use her life to express my own, or even to understand it better. I am relieved that we have begun to talk about all these complicated and subtle things.

Sandy
April 19

MY FORTY-EIGHTH BIRTHDAY. This morning, as I sat at the kitchen table drinking coffee, Barbara heavily climbed the back stairs from the yard, wordlessly extending her hand in which she held one yellow iris. In the years we have been together, her vegetable garden has been turned into a place where she grows flowers for me—her first, a purple iris. My eyes filled, as did hers, and we were silent, the spring flower at the center of our joined hands, connecting us.

Later in the day Barbara asked me to accompany her as she went for her first haircut in thirteen months. Her hair was coming out again, catching in the teeth of her comb, after having grown in during the summer of radiation. She had allowed the sparse tufts to grow wild on her head. Like a once-well-tended garden blighted by a storm, she purposefully did not groom it, but sadly watched it continue to thin and fall out.

In the salon Barbara stared at herself in the mirror, watching intently as her hair resumed a short, gamine shape and her delicate face reemerged from the tangle that had obscured it. Feeling lovely again, she relaxed under the soothing hands of the hairdresser.

We went across the street to our favorite cafe to celebrate my birthday and to anticipate our first trip to Europe. We basked in each other, in the sweetness of the moment, the dozen oysters now a familiar centerpiece on the table between us.

Sandy
April 29

AMSTERDAM. It is not quite spring. The tulips at the Keukenhoph Garden did not open naturally but were forced in hothouses the better to serve the greedy eyes of tourists. I find myself drawn to the early images of Van Gogh, the hollow-eyed, tubercular peasants, more than to the blazing light in his later work. I notice graffiti on the ground and forget to look up towards the gabled rooftops. I'm anxious, feel responsible for Barbara's health, strength, spirits, good time. I am too vulnerable to her, trying to be so perfect.

My own mood swings are extreme: wishing sometimes to be at home; at others, delighted by Barbara's glee in each new experience; and at yet still other times, I want to be quietly alone. My life feels taken over by Barbara's needs and illness and money. I feel suffocated, protective, raw, and filled with love for her—from one moment to the next. All the time.

Barbara
May 3

An absolutely wonderful day, as all these days have been. I bought a pair of green European loafers and a green cashmere coat. Earlier in the day Sandy and I went to the Van Gogh Museum and my understanding of his greatness increased and deepened a hundredfold. His signature is so unique in the history of painting, so able to incorporate and transcend both the derivative (Japanese) influence and impressionism around him into a visionary and abstract place. His earlier, darker, somber Dutch works are very moving. The *Potato Eaters*, especially.

I seem to be doing very well except for my vertigo which is controlled by Meclazine. I could allow myself to get depressed about it but I don't because I don't want it to inhibit my activities. It is mainly frightening, not uncomfortable. My energy seems good, except that I fall asleep rather easily every afternoon. I merely shut my eyes and I'm out.

Today I feel angry at my cancer. This is just the beginning. This is the first trip Sandy and I have made together to Europe, the first of what I hope will be many, and I am furious that I can see limits. I hate it. My hair continues to fall out. I continue to gain weight. My skin continues to flake off. I still continue to have nausea and my vertigo continues and I'm on constant medication.

Barbara
May 6

Sandy is crying very sadly and I'm a bit numb on this return flight home. After a few days in Paris, after a special train ride from Amsterdam, I wanted to stay longer—just a few weeks longer.

Sandy
May 6

Last night, after a splendid day at Sainte Chapelle, Notre Dame and a three-hour lunch at the four-star Tour D'Argent, I couldn't fall asleep. I felt Barbara beside me, heard her breathing as we lay on the lumpy bed in our rooftop room, her hair so thin, her frail skull again exposed, hands worrying, tugging at her hair even in her sleep. The image of her hair, patches of scalp re-emerging is the omnipresent reminder of the thinning, the diminution of time, of the possibility for a full, luxuriant life together. Yesterday I wrapped her head in a scarf and tied it with a rakish bow—only we both knew it was a mask, not a decoration.

Last night I lay beside her so lonely and so desperate. I wanted to stay and tempt her with museums, culture, food. Tempt her with life until we tricked the process of disease with such joy and abundance of love and adventure it would simply disappear.

I feel unimaginable sadness at thinking of myself without her. She is like a weed that persists in pushing up through the concrete of her circumstance. She sees the smallest flower, the most delicate detail. She hungers to learn all the languages, the food, the history, and culture everywhere she goes. She evokes in me a sense of pressing against the light, striving to see, to taste, to smell, to experience.

We sit beside each other on this plane taking us back, bent over our journals, writing to each other—and to ourselves.

Sandy
June 3

I have returned home drained from a week working on the road. Barbara finds my travel very emotionally disruptive and things are strained between us. Each word seems to reverberate in the air, shimmering and hanging there, weighed for hidden meanings, potential hurts or slights. We are guarded and tentative with each other.

Barbara
June 4

The neighbors whose backyard faces ours—the ones with the dog who barked all night and with whom our dog had "conversations"—have moved. I feel very sad. Not that I knew them so well, but because any change is hard. I feel sad for Sembei, our dog. No more ritual barking with her old friend.

Sandy
June 6

Barbara alternates between wanting me on the road engaged in my own life or at home engaged with her. Everything is unpredictable and some days are a seesaw of conflicting needs that change hourly: her uncertainty about taking sabbatical time without clearly defined work; her discomfort with a body that is swollen with edema and growing weaker, leaving her unable to do very much without needing to rest; her mixed loyalties to her parents and sister; her feeling that she has too many friends who need her to need them. All this makes me want to protect her, from too much choice, too many possibilities.

Now, in this interim time, she fills her days with book reviews and new editing clients. It is unclear whether these will sustain her. It is a difficult time and I feel quite unable to do much but look on helplessly.

Sandy

June 7

Deena wondered if Barbara and I were organizing our lives around her dying rather than our living. "How would you both be different in the relationship if you knew she would be alive for ten years? How would the relationship be different?" she asked us. Thinking about that question and the implications it raised for the way we have been living has been quite sobering. We have been racing around filling ourselves up. While it was fun, it was also pressured and frantic. We both need to slow down.

Barbara

June 8

My own job ends soon, precisely one month from today and I feel frightened and melancholy. Despite my choice to ask for a leave of absence, it feels like I am being forced out. Despite my longing for free time, I fear I will have too much of it. Despite my yearning for unfettered thoughts, I'm afraid that the lack of structure my job provides will put me in constant touch with the finiteness of thoughts, of life. I must move now towards a life filled with the melancholy of "necessary losses."

Sandy

June 10

Barbara has decided to create a small counseling practice for women who have been recently diagnosed with breast cancer. While I'm supportive of this decision and admire her greatly for making it, I feel so deeply weary. My skill in watching my words, weighing the emotional impact of what I say, has become like a pencil point sharpened finer and finer until it is about to break. I need now to be gathered in where it is warm, where there are murmurs of women, where I don't have to be smart or brave or interesting or patient or sensitive. Just for a while.

Letter from Barbara
June 14

Dear Friends,

So much has happened to me since my last letter to you that I scarcely know where to begin. There has been so much change, both in my external circumstance and within myself, that I feel like a pilgrim finding my way.

In October my malpractice suit was settled out of court for a substantial amount of money. The reason I won it so quickly is that the facts were depressingly clear: the length of my life has been substantially shortened. I was the winning loser.

In December I took a trip with Sandy to Australia and New Zealand and began to live as I had never lived before, taking more risks and chances. I learned that living is risking, facing and mastering fears. I was always afraid to drive on the left side of the road. Well, I did it and got into a terrible skid during a New Zealand thunderstorm. Had there been more traffic on the road, it would have been a serious accident. But this skid gave me more courage and freedom to try other things, like snorkeling. I was always afraid I wouldn't breathe right and would choke. But I tried and now I'm a snorkeling fan, having discovered the most exquisitely colored and delicately shaped world beneath the surface. I am no longer afraid of most things. Least of all, really living.

During January and February I began to write about the irony of having a shortened lifespan and lots of money. I was asked to write a paper for a book on how sociologists look at their illnesses. It was an important paper because I began to write in a new way, with my personal writing fully integrated with a social analysis. It became clear to me that I wanted to write things that moved the reader, that were not just "smart" articles. I am building upon this kind of writing by looking at other areas, for example, what it feels like to be on the receiving end of medical technologies. I am experimenting with mood, voice, tone, and style. It's very liberating and a deeply feelingful way of writing.

In the spring I had a one-year anniversary party on the date of my diagnosis. It was a day of great sadness and firm determination to make everything count more. I decided to take a medical leave from work for a year. By late spring, on the day I received a letter confirming my tenure, I submitted my letter for one year's leave of absence commencing July 1, 1986. For the next five months I'll still be on chemotherapy. After that, when I go off chemotherapy, I will have other things to deal with. I feel afraid. Will my body fight the cancer on its own? Is the cancer going to come back without chemotherapy? How soon? How much time do I really have?

In general, though, I am looking forward to this year with great joy, as a time to write, travel, listen to music, read, and do everything. I want to pack each day full of life, make the volume of time expand, make every moment more intense, make every laugh come from deeper in the gut, meet every person with an open heart, live with zest.

Though the side effects of chemotherapy are cumulative and consequently more difficult for me, I continue to be psychologically very whole and essentially happy. I get more tired now. I need to rest several times each day, usually after each activity. Sometimes I can't concentrate because I feel so exhausted that it's hard to read during my rest periods. Yet, on some days, I'm full of energy and never rest at all. It's unpredictable and I have to live from moment to moment, assessing hourly as I go along. My cancer teaches me to be exactly in the present, right in the moment, and nowhere else.

I continue to be happy, cheerful, excited, eager to live a full and rich life. I love nature movies on PBS, watching how whales make sounds and chimps communicate, how insects move about. I love my garden, the walks I take with my dog, seeing the neighbors and kvetching about the neighborhood. It is a time of loving my friends and sharing important experiences for us to treasure. It is a time of great joy and love, an unexpected gift in spite of—or perhaps because of—this cancer.

Be well *und zei gezunt,*

THE EMPTY LADDER

Sandy

We fight less often now. The specter of invisibility no longer my insistently familiar demon. Barbara, too, has softened, her tolerance for sharing me with others expands. I remember our arguments with fondness. We fought with an innocence that there would be endless time to work through all our knotted-up places. To process, confront, let things settle, talk again. We believed in a far side. In resolution.

For both of us the deepest wound was the hunger to be seen. To be heard. To be understood. My judgments, her sarcasm. My righteousness, her ambivalence. We teetered on the edge of our pasts, in therapy and at kitchen table marathons, drinking endless pots of tea, emptying boxes of Kleenex, with doggedness.

My style of fighting was flamboyant, dramatic, noisy. I would slam doors, make ultimatums, hiss pronouncements. Barbara pulled in, closed off, withheld, and hid, leaving me outside her, alone, bereft.

One night after reaching an impasse in a fight we had been having for hours, one in which both of us were convinced the other was totally unreasonable, I announced firmly, "I'm going to sleep in the other room. We can continue this in the morning. Perhaps if we sleep on it, we can find some other way to settle it." With that, I gathered my bathrobe, swept off down the hall, and slammed the door.

Five minutes later Barbara's face appeared at the window, perched on a ladder she had propped up against the side of the house. "I wouldn't come through a closed door, but you didn't say anything about a window," she said with a playful smile. Our fight fell away in that unexpected moment. She climbed in through the window, leaving the ladder propped against the house until we removed it together in the morning.

During our second year together, returning from a party, I was determined to make Barbara understand that when she challenged me in a political discussion in a group of her friends, I felt humiliated, unprotected and hurt. I strode up and down the hall, talking loudly, making my point over and over again. The more insistent I became, the more silent and watchful she was. I grew panicky and my voice rose as I prepared to argue my case yet again. She walked up to me, and as I was trying to be my most formidable, put her hand on my cheek and said quietly, "Sandy. It's only me, Barbara."

I began to weep then and sank to the hallway floor. Barbara knelt beside me, gathering me into her arms and rocked me as I wept for the child who had been railing at ghosts for decades.

Once, after a fight about dust under the bed, dirty dishes in the sink, my articles lost and buried under piles of folded socks, dishtowels, and a new dog collar, I announced, "That's it. I can't think in this chaos. This relationship is a mistake. I'm leaving." I flung open the front door and paused on the landing, wondering where I was going to go. Barbara brushed past me, walked quickly to my car, and jumped up on its hood.

"You're going? Then you're taking me with you. We're talking," she insisted. "I'm lying on this car until we talk this through. This is not about housework. I simply don't believe it no matter how many times you keep saying the same thing."

I relievedly stormed into the house, going directly to the kitchen table to await her, arms firmly folded across my chest, heart smiling at the sight of her sprawled across my car.

Our fights were most often about Barbara's alternating need for me and her need of privacy for herself, longing for our connection and feeling overwhelmed by it. I, so attuned to her responses, scanned her for impatience, irritation, the dangerous moment when a cutting word or dismissive gesture would cast me out.

My life as a public person was always hard for Barbara. The leave-taking, the coming home after being away for four or five days, the long-distance phone calls from endless motel rooms were all disruptive and anxiety producing. Barbara was angry when I left and angry when I came home. She would have preferred that I worked near our home, leaving at the same time each morning and returning predictably for dinner each night. That way, she could have the house all to herself during the day, and me all to herself in the evening.

But after the diagnosis, Barbara's anger at the absence of predictability, order, the certainty of a carefully orchestrated series of days, months, years was directed at the hospital, the technicians, the health care system—anything and anyone who got in her line of vision. She threw herself into the lawsuit with a vengeance I had never before seen in her.

"I have a fantasy," she whispered one night, "that the day before I die, I'll strap dynamite all over my body and go and stand in front of the hospital and blow myself up. I hate them." Then she began to cry with despair and exhausted rage.

This single focus worked for awhile. The lawsuit brought to a boil what had been simmering in her. The injustice, the economics of health care, the politics of life and death. Her experience opened her to all the women who, like her, had had poor medical care, had trusted a system that was structurally and, at times, personally unresponsive to their needs. She mobilized her anger. She raised funds for the National Women's Health Network. She spoke out and joined organizations to educate and inform women. And as always she wrote. It was not just her anger now. It was about justice.

Our fighting has nearly evaporated, become unnecessary, now that life and death is our consuming urgency. Barbara and I understand there will not be time to work through all our wounded places and the ways we were abrasive to each other.

Our early fights seem so far away now. Not that the reasons are gone but the hope for resolution is. How could either of us trust resolution? We've gone as far as we will ever go. Now our lives are about every day, every hour, each moment. The moments of tension surface—our eyes lock and voices grow tight—but now they are eased with a glance, a joke, a touch.

I am still jealous of Barbara's intimacies that leave little room for me—deep connections I can only observe from outside. I am afraid that she will die with regrets that will include me and our life together. I mute my irritation at her need to know and to control so much of every moment of our daily life—understanding that it comes from a profound sense of impotence and helplessness. Our prickly places chafe still, my travel particularly, but the carefully orchestrated balance of self and us will have to stand.

Now I have both my therapist, whose presence anchors me, and a support group, a gathering of women with whom I can allow myself the feelings that would be burdensome for Barbara. With them I can be irritated at Barbara's demands, can be self-absorbed about my loss of a partner, can romanticize her into "Saint Rosie" without fear of challenge or contradiction. These women have lost parents, brothers, friends, lovers, comrades. They have been in this place before me and are able to tolerate my restlessness, my terror, my despair, my rage. These women encircle me, listen, soothe, believe in, and love me.

Now the ladder is propped unused against the basement wall. No doors slam. No voices are raised. Instead our fight now is for meaning, for a maintained connection, for consciousness.

Taking Stock

August – December 1986

Sandy
August 6

I'll spend time with my family while Barbara travels to St. Croix with Peter and then on to New York for the sociology meetings. First a few days with my youngest daughter, Alison, then to Cape Cod with my eldest daughter, Janaea, then time at home with my mother in Boston, before Barbara returns. It will be a sort of processional, intersecting patterns unique to each twosome. Mothers and daughters.

I am missing Barbara terribly. Talking to her on the phone at the end of the day goes right through me. I so wish she were here, waiting for me in all the anonymous hotel rooms of my life. She is always the point of connection, the home. Walking into a hotel room where she awaits me, it becomes home.

Barbara
August 17

Today is a bad day: hourly (at least) hot flashes, back spasm, bad weakness, and fatigue. The word "wildfire" goes through my mind often. My greatest fear is wildfire cancer. The kind that consumes the chest wall, makes tumors in the ribs, goes to the liver and lungs and bones. I'm scared to death that I'm being kept alive with poisons.

Barbara
August 18

It is now forty-seven days into my year off and Sally gave me a massage during which she read positive affirmations such as "I am healed. . . . I am healthy." While she was saying these things, I had a vision of myself dying—being at home, slipping into a coma, feeling Sandy next to me, reading to me. And as I died, Sembei jumped on the bed and licked my face and, realizing that I was gone, whimpered away.

Then immediately after this image, I heard Jane's voice telling me how much life force I have and instantaneously I felt a rush of light, metallic silver, white in color, penetrating through and emanating from my being. It was pure, pulsating energy, vibrating wildly in my body, and it felt healing. When I returned to "normal," something was different, definitely different.

Two more times on chemotherapy, then off. I feel protected until October. As of now they have given me another year to live and maybe I'll have even more. Sandy says she thinks I'm healed. I hope she's right.

Barbara
August 23

I'm in New York now for the sociology meetings. I miss Sandy terribly and care so much about how she is doing in Boston. She works so hard. I woke up depressed, mainly missing home. My original purpose for being at the sociology meetings was to see everybody and show them I'm not dead. Now I could care less.

I went with Mom for her chemotherapy today and had the pleasure of showing her Balducci's food store in the Village. The necklaces I bought her look nice and please her.

Barbara
August 25

Whew! The conference has been nonstop. A whirlwind of people, asking me how I feel, telling me I look great, suggesting new books to read.

I can't remember when I have been angrier at my cancer. Sitting at the sociology meetings, hearing such mediocre papers, I vacillate from feeling mildly amused to being indifferent to being jealous. I hate my cancer. I hate what it's done to me. I, too, would like the luxury of sitting up there reading a mediocre paper. L. talking about how wonderful his new book is, the interviews he's doing on the subject of bodies! "I need a few cancer patients to round out the sample," he announces. People are so stupid about what they say!

I am angry at the casual phrases like "My job is killing me" and "You should live so long." There are very few people who can stay with hard stuff, not avoid, chatter, withdraw, or disappear. Sandy stays there. So do Jane and Linda. So does my sister. I'm very ready to go home. I had a wonderful talk with Sandy—she was very tender. It's hard for Sandy now, but it's the best I've ever been to her and for her. Centered, calm, and clear.

Sandy
September 5

We have both returned home. Barbara is ready to engage with the next order of business. We have been interviewing lawyers and finally chose one who is slow, meticulous, and exacting in her presentation of the options we have. It was a relief to have made the decision to work with her. It is so difficult to deal with all the exacting legal "ifs." If I die before Barbara. If her parents die before she does. If her sister dies before I do. All these eventualities need to be translated into a formal document. Barbara's last will and testament. Finally there doesn't seem to be any other choice.

Barbara
September 11

This morning I was bad. Did I have an adulterous affair? Did I masturbate with unfaithful fantasies? Did I hit someone, cause pain, harm, injury to another person? Was I neglectful of my dog? Did I not walk her and feed her properly? Did I spend my parents' money unwisely? Did I fail to water the garden, pick the tomatoes? No, none of the above.

I had a cup of coffee and a donut. And in the world where some things count and others don't, it's all strangely amusing. My weight is becoming more and more troublesome. I feel awful about it and the bloating is getting impossible.

Do you believe in miracles? Do you believe eating brown rice and steamed vegetables can increase my chances for a longer life? Or how about six glasses of carrot juice a day? Another cancer diet says a high intake of animal protein will help the immune system. Macrobiotics says animal protein will weaken, not strengthen, it. Whom to believe? What to believe? Each logic, on its own, sounds convincing. Macrobiotics wants to eliminate fat, water, and congestions of the organs in the immune system. Gerson wants to flood the body with vitamin A. That makes sense, too. Except no carrot juice is allowed on macrobiotics—it's too yin. These mutually exclusive diets drive me crazy. What to believe? When several diets agree, like no meat for instance, my beliefs are buttressed. And there is no evidence that diet makes any difference anyway, but I think that is myopia, as well as a measurement problem of Western medicine.

Shizuko told me my immune system is congested. If I go on macrobiotics, I will cure myself. You are what you eat. Cell structure, division, and growth are based on the environment you provide for them. She is the foremost macrobiotic nutritional adviser in America. A session with her costs $150 and it could be the basis of life change. She says I can beat the odds.

I had lunch in a macrobiotic restaurant and felt wonderful. My nose was clear and uncongested.

That same night I took friends for a nouvelle dinner and was immediately congested, had a migraine headache, had to take Ergomar and codeine tablets. So isn't the body saying something?

Barbara
September 16

I can't remember when chemotherapy has been worse than this. There is no letup. I wake up feeling like it's time to go to sleep. I'm in a hazy frame of mind, slightly nauseous all the time. Energy is very low, extremely low. Just writing this is hard: squeezing this pen between my fingers, holding it, feeling all the muscles in my arm tense to write tires me. I have at least two months of chemo to go and this may be the hardest part. All I want to do is lie down and it's only 10 a.m. It was this hard about six months ago, when I almost fainted after walking the dog for only ten minutes. Psychologically I force myself to have the courage to go through this.

To preserve joy and laughter in the midst of anguish, discomfort, and physical pain—a heroic vision indeed.

Barbara
September 21

Those last words seem so far away. I'm miserable, lonely, angry, bitter, and feel terrible. The chemo gets worse and worse and my energy is perhaps at its lowest. My spirit is low, too.

For the first time, I understand why people say "no" to chemo- therapy. It's not the vomiting or hair loss; it's the lack of energy. I can't walk a block without shortness of breath, can't get in a full day of activity. I have to lie down at one or two in the afternoon. I don't have enough energy to concentrate on reading, talking, thinking, and least of all, writing.

I'm not writing at all and that frightens me. I can't even remember what it is like to have a normal metabolism, normal energy, normal hair, and a normal body.

Watching the Emmys on TV, I am reminded how meaningful work is, how it eludes me now. I feel totally alone in my cancer. Alone in my agony. Alone in the pain.

Massage. Acupuncture. Herbs. Relaxation. What more can I do?

My life feels worthless, I feel depressed and I can understand wanting to die. H., in her work with people with AIDS, says many die angry. I'm trying not to. I'm trying to achieve completion. Maybe the strain is too much.

Sandy
September 22

Another shift. Barbara seems to be wearing down emotionally. She is eroding. Things are becoming too much for her to tolerate. Her mother fainted, fell, broke a vertebra, and is back in the hospital, and Barbara senses that this is the start of her mother's final decline. "I'm beginning to understand," she said to me last night, "that there can never be a turning back the clock. Even when I go off chemotherapy, when my hair grows back and I feel stronger, my mother may die. Or my father." I comfort her as best I can. Her heart is heavy and she clings to me, frightened about everything now. Bodies so fragile that there is the added danger of fainting, falling, and breaking. She yells at me if I pick up too sharp a knife. She worries when I return from an appointment later than expected. Danger is everywhere now and there is little comfort.

This is a very difficult time for me. I protect myself as well as I can by not making unnecessary social engagements and not demanding too much of myself. It seems to be working. Except for the matter of the unexpected sigh that escapes in its own rhythm—I find myself wondering, if the sigh were an exhalation/rush of words, what might they be?

Barbara
October 6

Today was the last day of my chemotherapy by injection. It is a wonderful and terrifying day. I alternate between feeling completely cured, never to see cancer again, and knowing that the statistical chances for a recurrence are quite high and that in sixty-five percent of the cases it hits the lungs first.

I'm scared shitless and feel very disoriented in my terror: sad, jubilant, out here on that ledge so far away, so steep, that if I were a dog or other animal I would be shaking uncontrollably almost all the time. That's how existentially anxious I am about living until this time next year. No—this time six months from now—without a recurrence, without cancer.

Sandy is a rock to me. I can depend on her and that keeps me together. She can also depend on me. I am a rock as solid as the earth for her. She's becoming more tender and more human, even sweet.

My eyes are teary. I have trouble swallowing because I am salivating so much. It's painful and uncomfortable. My body is puffy and bloated from all this chemo. But it's the end. The end of chemo. Hooray! Hooray! said with fear and trembling, but hooray nonetheless.

I must trust my body, trust it with all my might.

I am turning myself into someone who can wrap her body around a sword, an image I could hardly imagine two months ago. To wrap my body around a sword, around the physical discomfort in my neck, ribs, stomach—around the possibility of a recurrence.

Barbara
October 30

It is 11:30 p.m. and this is the second night in a row that I have taken a sleeping pill. I'm tired and exhausted, yet sleep does not take me over. I'm gripped and consumed by the fear. The fear. The fear of more cancer. The fear of going off chemotherapy. The fear of recurrence. The fear of not living because I'm afraid of dying. It's not anxiety, as in an anxiety attack, with its hot symptoms, raging away. It's fear. It's the fear of death, pure and simple. The fear of no time. Of claustrophobia. Of shrinking, shortened time. Of tragic regrets and the tragedy of life cut short; the tragedy of missed opportunities and the tragedy of having to live at the highs and lows, a roller coaster that few understand. It borders on my aloneness, that old aloneness that has haunted me for all my life.

I'm falling apart. During the year and a half of chemotherapy, I kept myself together, even cheerful, and had a good attitude. But now that it's over, I feel my grief acutely. It is relentless and I have troubles all the time. There are many troubles. There is bleeding from the nose. There is bleeding and intense anal pain. There is hypersalivation, retention of bodily fluids, and tears in my eyes that don't flow through the tear ducts but collect as if I had two sponges in those sockets. And there is the weight of my body, distended, misshapen, unfamiliar, irritable, uncomfortable, and unsexual. And unhappy. There is the dry skin. The difficulty swallowing. The black streaks in my nails. The funny sensations on my tongue. There are the skin cells on both my elbows that are hypertrophic, controlled now because of Methotrexate but bound to be inflamed and require therapy in a few months.

My hair keeps falling out in clumps again, coming out even as I run my fingers through it. It's really the thinnest it's been since chemo ended. Today I wore a hat for the first time in a year. That's how bad it looks.

And I am so weary, so unhappy, so afraid I won't even have three years. I watch the months pass, just like cliches in the movies that let you know how time passes: the leaves fall or the seasons change quickly or the pages of a calendar go flying.

I feel myself preparing for death: taking stock, making endings, providing for the people I love with money and property, creating financial trusts, and taking care of business.

I'm so afraid. I'm afraid of cutting myself with a knife in the kitchen. I'm afraid light bulbs will explode when I turn them on. I'm afraid all the dishes will fall on my head when I open the cabinet door to get a cup. I'm afraid the mice will run over my bare feet. It's everywhere. I don't know where the fear is, inside or out, and it's everywhere all the time.

I see so clearly who I am, what I am, what I stand for, who I might have become. I have made peace with parts of myself, forgiving some parts, still angry with others. I'm angry at an unfair, unjust, and incompetent, random world. I am in serious heartbreak, especially concerning my sister and Sandy. And my mother and father.

When I die, my friends' hearts will break in some way. They will know their aloneness even more. They will be reminded of what people do for passion and love. They will think of what it's like to be crazy in love and wonderfully mad and frenzied and happy, complete and wild with rage, smitten with unending sorrow, or obsessively involved. They will ask themselves why they didn't allow more of it in their lives.

Sandy
November 6

Barbara teaches me to see. To look into her death without flinching or turning away. Now that the chemotherapy has ended, she is frightened. Frightened that she is alone with her body, with the cancer. Frightened that there is little time.

But she is more than frightened. She is physically exhausted from the grueling assault her body has experienced. Bloated, constantly tired, nauseous, sore. Her body has been battered and she feels it as a stranger's body when she most needs to embrace it as her own. Forgive it. Love it.

Now I am back at work, helping other women to see. To look into their lives without flinching or turning away.

I notice my own body beginning to age. My neck seems suddenly to have become lined. My face has crosshatching marks when I awaken. My eyes need stronger and stronger glasses. My ears cannot hear without an aid. My body feels unfamiliar, and I too must learn to embrace it. Forgive it. Love it.

Letter from Barbara
December 1986

Dear Friends,

It has been about two months since I've been off chemotherapy and these have been among the worst since I was diagnosed with cancer almost two years ago. Despite the terrible side effects, almost steady fatigue, and depression, being on chemotherapy gave me the sense that I would not have cancer as long as I was taking my injections and tablets. I became what is known as a "chemo junkie."

At first I was elated that the symptoms were subsiding: no more nausea, no more bleeding, reduction of fatigue. I began jogging and then joined an aerobics class for senior citizens, figuring this was one population I could keep up with.

Shortly after I stopped chemo, I became phobic. Well, that's a shorthand way of describing a very complex process. I was afraid and yet did not experience my fear in a direct and clear way. On one occasion, just before turning on the switch of a reading lamp, I became terrified that the bulb would burst into a thousand pieces and they would fly into my face. At that moment I could feel the sensation of shrapnel-like torpedoes ripping into my face and could feel my skull being transformed into a thousand fountains of blood.

At night, when I tried to sleep, I became filled with free-floating anxiety, unfocused, contentless, and very disconnected from the frightening thoughts that seemed to occupy my days. So, day after day, I'd have fearful thoughts but would feel no emotion. And, night after night, I'd have wild fear but no thoughts to accompany them.

I knew from my years of psychotherapy that it would be helpful to relieve the panic by bringing together the thoughts and the emotions. One night, as I lay in bed, gripped by anxiety, I forced myself to imagine the worst thing that could happen to me: the cancer could come back. I imagined that my chest was full of tumors. I imagined feeling their hard, little forms. I scanned the surface of my skin and imagined a superficial, local recurrence, some errant cells needing surgical excision. I touched my right armpit with my left hand and imagined that I was feeling swollen lymph nodes. And then I finally imagined the unthinkable: that it was in my neck, travelling up my spinal column into my brain. Slowly I took a deep breath. I had thought the worst. I began to cry with a deep sadness that I now know resides in me, with which I have an uneasy partnership. After being brave and courageous through a year and a half of treatment, I wept for an interrupted life, for the relentless rage I have about the malpractice, and for the tragedy of an unfinished agenda.

Finally I cried for myself. And just like in an exorcism, the panic began to lift, the fear drifted away, and I was left drained but cleansed. Freedom, precious freedom, comes in so many forms.

For this year I celebrate my freedom from fear, the virtues of serenity and security. I celebrate my toughness of mind and spirit, the ability to conquer fear without becoming hardened and thus compromising tenderness. I celebrate my connectedness with my family, my zany nephew, and my partner, Sandy, whose optimism I've relied on during many dark days. She has been my foundation, my grounding, my base. I celebrate all the lessons cancer has taught me, all the inner freedoms I am discovering, and all the webbings of life that give the necessary illusion of terra firma, so that a person can take one step. And then another.

I celebrate the vastness, the largeness, the growing expansiveness and spaciousness of the person I have become, the largeness of my heart, and the depth of my understanding.

It is so incredibly wonderful to be alive.

Remember.

With love,

THE WILL

Barbara

I've just finished reading the final version of my will. It's 11:30 p.m. Sandy is sleeping in the other room and the house is still. I glance across the room and see my dog sleeping in Sandy's father's old brown leather reading chair.

My will. A codified, legal document. The crystallization, the representation of my wishes. I never thought I'd have any money to divide. I never believed in accumulation and savings, just a pension for my old age. Now I have money. Medical malpractice money. Blood money.

Sandy

Neither of us ever had any money. Both of us worked for wages. Barbara was raised in a marginally working-class family and had been expected to enter the postal service. Safe, secure work, her father told her. Benefits. Pension. Security. But she became an academic.

I worked as a secretary while raising my children. Now that they are grown, I am a counselor and workshop leader. For the seven years we have lived together, we have always contributed equally into our household account. We meticulously added expenses at the end of each month, gathering receipts from the manila envelope stuck behind the kitchen door. We would sit together at the kitchen table with a pocket calculator, add the bills (which seldom exceeded $600), and divide them equally, with the exception of a separate accounting of long-distance telephone calls. Then we would exchange checks and drink tea.

Barbara

The Kaiser doctors told me that the lump I showed them was not suspicious. Even as it grew, and I returned for a second evaluation, the doctors assured me that nothing was wrong. But I was alarmed and insisted upon a mammogram. Negative. No problem. And even when my right breast was twice the size of the other, the third doctor I saw, a surgeon, told me to stop drinking caffeine. No single, individual doctor in the Kaiser system caught it. And because of their collective incompetence, I am going to die within the year, at the age of forty-four or forty-five, depending on how I can stretch the time from this moment.

And because of their incompetence, and because I was furious enough to fight, I got a malpractice settlement for $296,000. All in one check.

Sandy

It was a series of appalling mistakes. The breast cancer had already invaded her lymphatic system. Barbara was consistently misdiagnosed and given inadequate care. I watch her undergo painful treatments, adjust to new limitations, and face her own death. I am stunned by the magnitude of my rage and my approaching loss. I feel powerless as Barbara struggles for her life. And now we face the outlandish reality of more money than either of us has ever imagined.

Barbara

I hate this money, this goddamn blood money, that comes from years taken from me. As if it could ever make up for the negligence and unfairness of it all. I hate the disease. I hate how my life has turned into a series of appointments in doctors' offices, CAT scans, blood tests, chemotherapy, and its side effects. Am I supposed to say, "$2,000" every time they stick a needle in me? Is every experience of throwing up worth $1,000? This money is supposed to make up for my shortened life and the extraordinary emotional pain that comes with the consciousness of that fact. This money is supposed to compensate me for the physical pain I had to endure, the hospitalizations, the morphine shots. This money is supposed to compensate me for the loss of a normal life.

Ever since the day of my diagnosis, I've had to reshuffle the ordinary balance of attention between self and other. Ever since that day, I've had to become more self- absorbed, more inward. I have learned to constantly take inventory. I lost my sense of proportion, my sense of a normal life. Am I supposed to have a meter ticking away each time something terrible happens to me, financially evaluate it, and see if it all adds up to $296,000?

Sandy

She cries each time they draw blood. Little, childlike whimpering sounds that she tries to mask with apologetic jokes. I cry at sentimental television programs. We are both edging toward our own feelings with the same halting steps. Unable to deal directly with the overwhelming reality of this disease, we find smaller, more tolerable ways to experience our grief.

Barbara

During the few months that followed, I tried to wrest pleasure from this grotesque circumstance. We travelled, bought leather furniture, custom-made tables, botanical and architectural engravings, even designed a rug while in New Zealand and had it shipped. Unable to fabricate the desire for any more objects, it finally became clear to me that we could never spend all this money. I had to face the fact that money would remain after I died. I would need a will.

Sandy

One night at dinner time, Barbara told me she was preparing to draw up a will and wanted to discuss her feelings about it and its provisions with me. Unable to respond, I busied myself with getting dinner on the table, my mind racing as I tried to sort out all the feelings her matter-of fact pronouncement stirred in me. It was real now. She needed to prepare for her death. She would die. I would be alone. We wouldn't grow old together. Short, staccato-like thoughts that slid away only to be quickly replaced by others. Unable to hold on to any one feeling, my mind was filled with kaleidoscopic images and I sat down heavily on the kitchen chair and began to cry. I tried several times to postpone the discussion, saying that I wanted a bit of time to sort out my own responses and the need for us to talk about this. Gently and firmly Barbara kept returning to our need to face the financial aspect of her illness and approach it in the same way we approached everything else. Clearly, truthfully, and lovingly.

We began to talk haltingly about what she wanted to go in her will and how we would proceed to find a lawyer that would be responsive to the fact that we are a lesbian couple. We would proceed through this inevitable task as we had all the others: preparing paperwork for insurance coverage, notifying colleagues of changed plans, interviewing surgeons. Barbara reminded me that we had done all that together; we could do this as well. Still unable to formulate a reply, having forgotten to eat dinner, I began to clear the table and do the dishes.

Almost at once I began to think about this money, dream about it, calculate it and the divisions that Barbara had initially proposed. I began to recognize the unstated expectations I had unconsciously formed about this money. For Barbara it represented time she would no longer have, while for me it was an unexpectedly complex series of assumptions I had never articulated to myself or to her. I had unconsciously taken for granted that Barbara's having money would mean that I, too, would have money. The fact that I had continued to work, travel, give workshops, and see clients was an expression of my own work identity, my own political urgencies, my own autonomy, my own need to keep a part of my life for myself. In addition to assuring me that there was more to my sense of myself than the couple identity of Sandy and Barbara, my work was personally gratifying. But since Barbara had received her settlement, my work never again had the same financial immediacy. And now I was facing the fact that Barbara's having money meant no more and no less than that. It was hers, to do with as she saw fit. She might spend it all on travel or art work, on her family or political organizations. It was her decision and had nothing at all to do with me. I felt defenseless, jealous, and surprisingly angry.

Barbara

I approached the will like I approach everything else in my life: slowly, steadily, and methodically. I always collect lots of data and ask people questions. In effect, I do a little survey. I establish the boundaries of the range of possibilities and then I locate a place on that continuum that's comfortable for me. I always take a rational, problem-solving approach to things. This was no different. It didn't seem to be about emotions, feelings, relationships, or obligations. For me it was about doing it "right," and that meant fairly and justly.

I drew a line down the center of a yellow pad and put the words "money" and "symbolic" at the head of each column. Under "symbolic" I wrote friends' names and decided what objects I wanted each one of them to have. Under "money" my task was to figure out the percentages that would go to the important people in my life.

Sandy

What are the percentages of loving? How would I translate respect, value, support, ideology, years spent, shared history into ratios? But that is, of course, what Barbara needs to do—for her will translates the language of the heart into that of a bloodless, legalistic document. During all these weeks, I have not yet made my feelings about this process of allocation explicit. I could not tolerate my own yearnings, my own needs to be chosen as the most important person in her life. Some part of my feeling of loss had to do with understanding that preparing a will would be quite a different matter if I had remained in my traditional, heterosexual marriage of the 1950s. There would be fewer choices, more certainty, and more unquestioned priorities. But we had both chosen lives that would not tolerate such assumptions. I knew she had a family—a recently married younger sister whom she had helped raise and whom she still protects fiercely and loyally, an infant nephew, aged and frail parents, and close friends. I knew all this but had not allowed myself the dangerous experience of thinking about what it might mean.

"A will is not a negotiable document. These are my wishes," she muttered when I read the first draft of her will and began to question some of its provisions. I recognized that I would not be "well taken care of" in the distribution of her assets. Her parents, sister, and political commitments were going to siphon off what could potentially come to me. I had come to think of this as my blood money. My trade-off for the loss of my beloved partner. If I wasn't going to have Barbara, I wanted all the money that had come to represent her life.

Barbara

I don't want to leave anyone anything. The only reason I'm doing it is because I have a sense of obligation to my family and to Sandy. I hate this money. I hate every dollar. I have the image that all the dollars are stuffed inside my stomach cavity and I am pregnant with money. I can feel their hands dipping into this cavity and taking out handfuls of blood-soaked dollars.

I am ashamed of these feelings, of not wanting to leave any money to my important people. I don't want anyone to have a good time with my money. I'd sooner give it away to groups and organizations whose work I support, who do good things in the world. This blood money is in need of redemption and good works is the only way I can imagine redeeming.

Sandy

I listen to her plans for giving this money away and recognize for the first time how much I resent having to share this blood money with anyone else. How much I resist any feelings of generosity when this process is predicated on my losing her. How much my heart closes around not "having," not "getting," not "being cared for." I was faced with the task of confronting aspects of myself that were carefully masked, guarded, or denied. I had to encounter the infantile, jealous, terrified, competitive, scared Sandy. While I understood that I was not going to allow myself to act upon these feelings or this new knowledge of myself, I knew that I needed to face them squarely. I struggled with my proprietary attachment to Barbara, allowing little room for her love of and need for others. I faced my bitterness when I recognized my patterns of self-denying generosity that left me with few financial resources as I approached fifty. I longed for, but feared, financial dependency. I tried to balance my need to be "special" with the sense of belonging her family has offered me. I remind myself of the meanings of this life that could never be reduced to codicils and clauses.

Barbara became my teacher in this process. I could not allow myself to be less than what she was insisting upon for herself. Wanting to keep my autonomy and my independence while at the same time allowing myself to be financially supported was a dichotomy that was both mutually antithetical and one I heartily disapproved of in myself. Having generosity of spirit—sharing my ideas, accomplishments, and money with others—was one of my best qualities and one that Barbara both admired and emulated. I was, however, faced with the irony that there also existed deeply rooted inside me a set of traditional feelings that were completely at odds with my carefully constructed and thought-out feminist politics. I wanted Barbara to ask me, "How would you like to spend the time we have remaining to us? How can I make your dreams possible?" I wanted her to keep me at home during this final period of her illness. To allow me to care for her—to play with her—to travel with her and not worry or even think about making a living. Now that there was enough money, why should I have to work?

I reminded myself of all the conversations during our courting days when we passionately agreed that our partnership (and indeed all good partnerships) should be formed by two independent people who join to build a life together on a foundation of competence and economic self-sufficiency, generated by work based on care and passion. We assured each other that we were women who would make autonomous decisions about how, where, and when to spend our money.

But how can I now feel like the most important person to her if that fact is not reflected in her financial decisions? What if it had been me who had cancer? How would I have divided my money among Barbara and my children? My political commitments? Wouldn't I have found myself struggling similarly with ratios, percentages, choices? Wouldn't I have to evaluate individual life against political need? Collective use against private gain?

The other irony is that even if she had not won the malpractice suit, even if we had no money except our weekly salaries, I would still have made the same choices and would live exactly as I do now. I chose to cancel my workshops across the country to be at home with her. I chose to reduce my income in order to free up the time that would allow me to be with her. I made that decision quickly and clearly, without conflict or sense of sacrifice. But I am still left with confusion about the meaning this money has for me. Do I need proof that she appreciates my choices? That I mean the most to her? Still, even while berating myself for these responses, I have felt jealous, angry, and hurt that she appears to care more about other people than she does about me. The feeling embarrasses me and is surprising in its intensity. I castigate myself for constructing an equation that makes money equivalent with caring. I feel ashamed of myself and unable to stop the feelings that flood me. I hold the intrusive thoughts in abeyance, but they intrude. Again and again.

Barbara

Under the column headed "money," I begin with my history. I have always given ten percent of my income to organizations that reflect my social values. So the first step was clear. In my will I had to continue the tradition of giving to others. Not everything would go to my sister or Sandy or my parents. But I still had to figure out the other ninety percent. It is a problem of translation, I tell myself, a problem of numerical representation: how to express in legal language what I experience as a deeply interconnected, dense, cross-referenced narrative that holds together a number of values and principles.

I began by examining how I had lived. I reviewed my history to uncover the consistent and deep values that had informed my decisions. I reminded myself that I always talked about books, art, music, and movies. I remembered that the most satisfying conversations combined emotional intensity, cultural themes, and intellectual analysis. I always had lots of records and books but never too many clothes. It became clear to me that the primary values by which I had lived my life centered on intellectual and psychological development. I became a teacher, a profession that embodied these values. Now these same values are reflected in a trust fund that provides an education for my sister's children.

My mother had a second-grade education and has suffered from illiteracy all her life. She was unable to hold a job because she couldn't read, write, or add numbers fast enough. But though she reads slowly, she understands complex ideas. My father, who, now half blind, still hunches over the *New York Times* every day with his magnifying glasses, gave me a legacy of precision—in language, measurement, and thought. It was my father who measured my childhood handwriting with his drafting instruments to make sure the letters were equally sized and properly formed. Both my parents gave me their deep love (and awe) of education and learning.

Towards them I have a sense of obligation. I want to make sure that they are as comfortable as possible in their old age. And for them I created another trust fund, so they could live out their lives with as much intellectual stimulation and physical comfort as money can buy.

Once I had articulated my basic values, I could consider how much money each person needed. I could hear my father's voice, repeating Marx, "From each according to ability, to each according to need." But when I thought about who among my beneficiaries really needs money, the answer was no one. Yet in another sense, everyone needs surplus cash. Who among my beneficiaries can't use a few extra bucks to have a vacation, buy a better stereo, save for a child's future, have an education? Make a dream come true?

Sandy

"What will you do after I'm dead?" she asks me tentatively.

"I don't know, why are you asking me?" I reply, shocked and frightened by the question.

She becomes angry and explodes, "Because I'll be damned if you're gonna spend this money with someone else. Or buy a house. I don't want you and my sister to have luxuries as a result of my death. I'd rather give it all away!"

I pause, wondering what I plan to do with this money, this blood money, however much it turns out to be. How can I spend it in a way that will honor its origin? We sit together late at night, huddled together on the gray sofa, and alternately talk and cry about my life after her death. About our painful acknowledgment that there will be an "after" for me. She tells me of her desire to provide that which I never had: a rigorous education. As a single mother, and even after my daughters were grown, I continued to live in the service of others, never creating the time or resources just for myself—to think, to write, to move from emotional work to the more clear-edged world of the intellect. She encourages me to remember that old longing, those old dreams.

I feel lightheaded as we talk. It feels somehow like a piece of theater. Here we are, two healthy looking, sturdy, middle-aged women playing roles. One is pretending to be a dying woman and the other, her loving partner. I tell her, "This just doesn't seem real to me. You just don't seem sick." But then I begin to sob because her sickness is all too real. It is under the surface, not visible but centrally determining. It cannot be seen or felt or stopped, but it is the center, now, from which all our decisions are made.

"Yes," I tell her much later, tears spent. "You're right. I think I would like to go back to school."

I lie with my head in her lap as she strokes my hair. We had talked for so many hours during our years together about my hunger to learn, about my desire for a more traditional education, about my ache for her to guide me through the books, the discussion, the intellectual subtleties she so relishes.

"I think I would like to use whatever money is left to me to study, to write, to learn. It would be both a reflection of my desire and a way to honor your life. Also it'll help me get through the next period of time, however long it takes for me to learn to be alone again."

Her face softens and she takes me into her arms. "Yes. Yes, that's perfect. It is everything that matters to me. Everything I care about. To spend this money on your education sounds right to me. To make your dream come true."

Understanding we have come to an ending, we stop and look carefully at each other's faces. Gently we smile with pride in our accomplishment. Hand in hand we tenderly lie down in bed, wrap ourselves around each other, and go to sleep.

I'm coming to understand some of the larger meanings embedded in the process of creating this will. I have been forced to turn and face parts of myself that have lived silently and invisibly, powerfully determining, precisely because they were unacknowledged. I have begun to learn how the public values I had espoused often masked the private feelings I have denied. I have begun to allow the blending of the public and the private self, both in this process with Barbara as well as in my relationships to work, to my family, and within our community.

I have seen Barbara send and receive stirring personal letters to friends and colleagues across the country, articulating the nature and meaning of their relationships. I have participated with the women who formed our healing circle which first met a year ago to hear Barbara's diagnosis. As they did then, they continue now to provide love, support, and a telephone tree. Together we have created a re-birthday celebration on February 22, a gathering where we consciously honor living, with champagne, laughter, and tenderness.

My life with Barbara represents the most open, trusting, and emotional relationship I have ever had. She has taught me many things and is leaving me a legacy that will provide a stable and lasting foundation for the rest of my life. I have been blessed with one hundred percent of her time, devotion, courage, sense of humor, and passion. I have been with her during full and rich years and have flourished in her love. I have stretched and seen her do the same, both of us moving in directions and on paths we never would have been brave enough to choose alone. We have both learned what it means to love fully, unquestioningly, and unstintingly; for there is, finally, no other way to love.

And when she leaves, it is not a percentage of herself she leaves, but all the tastes, smells, melodies, and sensations of our loving.

Barbara

There it is, all proper and legal. There are many things wrong with it already. If I did it again, I'd give away much more money to groups whose work I support. I'd change things around a little bit, endlessly refining it. But on the whole, these are my values: to be of service, to work to liberate others from ignorance, poverty, and despair, to help others discover their own possibilities. And these basic values, the ones that have shaped my life, are now legally codified, these passions of a well-examined, well-lived, well-spent, and well-loved life.

Ritual and Ceremony

January – February 1987

Sandy
January 1

The year begins with a heightened sense of urgency. Now we race from precipice to precipice. A phone call from Dr. Grant on December 31 tells us that Barbara's recent tests reveal that cancer has now invaded her liver. We again plunge into assessing the pros and cons of treatment options, filling yellow pads with unfamiliar words, statistics, probabilities, and side effects. After several consultations and second opinions, Barbara decides to have her liver directly infused with very strong chemotherapy, rather than continue with systemic treatment. It is a new and very painful treatment, requiring her to go into the hospital at once. Our decisions must be as rapid as the spread of the cancer; no time now for reflection.

"Let's go for it," she says resignedly. "There's not much to lose, and maybe some time to gain." I plan to stay in the hospital with her and I've arranged for a cot to be placed next to her bed so I can reassure both of us with my presence.

It has been less than two years since her diagnosis, less than one year since the rebirth party, a celebration designed to hold back the disease process, to affirm and insist upon life. I fear that without the documentation ritual provides, our lives together will be washed away like an elegantly constructed sand castle in the wake of this determined wave of cancer. We need to exhort the heavens, "*L'Chaim.* To life." We need to begin again.

Barbara

January 1

As I hold my breath until the liver procedure later this month, Sandy and I prepare for a ceremony of commitment, one she has wanted for years. I had hesitated, felt ambivalent, not comfortable with rituals. But each time Sandy and I have attended one, I have found myself unexpectedly moved, stirred by this creation of form, this reshaping of experience to envelop loved ones. Now with the gravity of my liver metastases, we both feel ready to create a ritual that will honor us, the life we have created together, and the community that rings and nourishes us. The time has come.

Once the decision was made, Sandy and I sat with Riek and Ingrid, who were visiting from Amsterdam, and with Berenice, here from New York, to plan together.

I was certain that I didn't want a traditional Jewish marriage ceremony as part of our joining. It felt conventional, and I feared it would become a social script—one that would feel removed from the spontaneous and deeply experienced connection that is our life together. I feared it would be something that we would have to fit ourselves into—like a lovely, old, ill-fitting cloak. To me it represented a narrowing of values, a singularity of cultural styles, rather than an expansion, an inclusion, a stretching that would reach into each heart, Jew and non-Jew alike.

As a child I had gone to a "non-sectarian" summer camp and I wanted to reflect those values in the creation of a service that would transform those who were strangers into an unexpected and joyous community. I needed universal symbols for that to happen, something to pierce each heart.

We discussed, considered, and evaluated possible elements to be included. It would be such a disparate group. Friends from my professional life as a sociologist. Political activists. Lesbian separatists. Heterosexual couples. Young, coupled, artistic women. Old lovers. New friends. So many varieties of people in our world; so many forms of building community. It worked for us. It had always worked for us. But now how did we create a ritual that would unify them and embody us? As we sat on the sofa sipping tea, our friends suggesting and weighing many ideas, an unexpected theme emerged.

We would begin the ceremony by ringing Tibetan bells and end it with *klezmer (freilach)* music. We would chant during the ceremony. Each guest would offer blessings to us. Unconsciously, without an articulated focus, Sandy and I found a way to join all the participants in community. We would use sound.

Sandy

January 2

Planning the ceremony of commitment has become an oasis of calm in the midst of this devastating medical news. In less than a week, our friends will gather to witness our love, to honor Barbara's courage in this time of shrinking possibilities, to dignify her insistence on a conscious death. I need the comfort of ceremony, the visibility of ritual, a way to honor who we are and what we have created in our lives as a couple. To insist upon being seen — something that as a lesbian couple we have never taken for granted. To stand proudly and name our relationship, what we have meant to each other, and the ways in which our lives brought people together.

Barbara and I decided that, in addition to the centrality of "sound," we want each guest to be an active participant in the day. Some have been asked to make a bolt of purple velvet into a *chupah* for us to stand beneath as we exchange vows. Others will prepare a scroll shaped like a Torah so everyone may inscribe their good wishes for us. Each guest will bring a flower, so that what results will blend color, shape, scent into an unexpected collective bouquet. And each loved one has been asked to prepare a blessing for the ceremony and a handkerchief to join us as we dance together at its conclusion.

Sandy

January 4

The ceremony began with the ringing of our Tibetan gong to signal the moment of gathering. As the sound slowly faded, our friends settled themselves onto chairs circling the living room. Jane lit a candle, reading first in Hebrew then in English, "We have come together to light this candle in honor of Sandy and Barbara's commitment. We bless them and hope for their happiness and well-being. Blessed be that which is holy. Amen."

Then Barbara, perched beside me on our kitchen counter, the place that now served as our altar, reached for my hand and spoke:

"This ceremony of commitment is the crystallization and public acknowledgement of the deep bond that we share today with our friends. We have both been reluctant during the past years to formalize our connectedness because of our ideological hesitations about using forms and traditions that did not fit our politics.

"But today we have found a way to create a ceremony that embodies all our deeply held values. It is traditional yet open; it is Jewish and it is also feminist, Buddhist, and pagan. It is about us as a couple but also as a couple whose identity is embedded in community, in friendship, in connectedness."

Turning to me, she continued, "Sandy, our relationship is one of the major accomplishments of my life. I came to understand so many things. I came to understand that the struggle to negotiate differences is itself a type of commitment. You have expanded my notions of a moral, ethical, and political life. You have made me feel beautiful and special, and I grew to become special to myself and to other people. I have learned what it's like to be loved unconditionally. That love has allowed me to let things build up inside myself, to let them accumulate into a whole self. In this relationship each of us, who had written separately before, found a way to write together, a way to blend, yet maintain a delicate separation. I celebrate this day as a culmination of all that we have created between us."

My eyes were wet with tears. Holding tightly to her hand, I turned to her and said, "Barbara, you have taught me much of what I have come to value about myself. You have helped me to think rigorously and clearly. You have taught me how to play and to sing 1930s medleys in the night. You have watched relievedly as I grew brave enough to look away from your wounds and towards my own. You have opened and softened my heart. In your love I have found a home. In your love I have created community and family. In your love I have learned to love myself."

Then Barbara turned from me to face those encircling us and said, "We face our future together with each one of you in this room. It is now the time of the biggest fight — of my life, for my life. You are my allies against despair and discouragement, against pain from disease. I will rely on all of you to be midwives in my passage and I consider myself blessed by your presence in my life." Barbara placed her hand in my lap, growing visibly tired but smiling with inexhaustible tenderness.

I added, "We have fought for each other. Our relationship has been tempestuous, vital, fierce, and passionate and has finally made us both whole. It is from this place of wholeness that we face our future together."

Then each guest was given a small glass filled with water as Jane explained, "Water is a holy essence, a medium for bathing as well as for blessings. Each of you in turn, holding this glass, may now offer your prayers and good wishes to Barbara and Sandy. After you have completed your benediction, please pour your water into this glass bowl in the center of the room. In it will be the mingling of the devotion, invocations, and wishes each of you have extended to them. We will again drink from this sacred bowl later in the ceremony."

Then our loved ones approached one at a time with their prayers. "I wish you the gift of time. You will stand today under the wings of the *Shekina*. May she bless your dwelling together."

"This ceremony is a memorable celebration of the profound bond between you. May it be a help in the painful times ahead."

"Your deep love has deepened my life."

"May you both love each other fiercely. I will be with you."

"Your love is like a *challah*. Even at night when you sleep underneath the white, embroidered cloth of your blanket, even in your dreams, your lives continue to braid together."

"It is a *mitzvah* — that you give this moment to us."

"I think of you both with grace and with dignity."

Words washed over us then, cleansing, healing, faces moist with tears and with love.

When the prayers were finished, Jane said, "We will now raise the *chupah*, with each of the four corners held by a significant woman in Sandy and Barbara's life. We ask them now to stand beneath it, to create a place together that symbolizes home, the sides open in welcome to all those who would enter and join them there. I ask you now to rise and form a circle around them. As the ring ceremony is held, we also will ring them in community."

Barbara slipped the ring onto my finger, placed her palm on my heart, and said, "This ring represents the unbroken circle of life and the completeness of our bond."

I reached out to touch her asymmetrical, narrow chest, decorated this day with purple silk.

"This ring symbolizes the delicacy and strength of Barbara as well as the delicacy and strength of our love."

Encircled by our friends, Jane then instructed everyone to close their eyes and exhale, allowing a breath to emerge, one that would surround us with light, with love, and with blessing. The room filled with the murmurs of "ommmm . . ." swelling and expanding as the sound grew louder, clearer, stronger. It filled us as we stood, our palms against each other's beating heart.

As the sound faded, each person then dipped their glass back into the ceremonial bowl as Jane continued, "We raise our glasses and in this moment sanctify this union, this commitment, this bonding. Congratulations."

As the enthusiastic cries of "*Mazel Tov! L 'Chaim!*" dissolved, they were replaced with another sound, old and familiar from Barbara's childhood. *Klezmer* music soared, joyously filling the air, as each guest held one end of a handkerchief, joined now with the person on either side of them. Thus connected we moved through each room of the house, dancing, filling the house with the energy, with the enthusiasm, with the holiness of this day.

Klezmer music finally gave way to rock and roll, blessed water to champagne, and the kitchen table filled with sushi and chocolates.

We danced, sang, delighted in each other, and the world that was ours.

Several hours later, when only a few women remained talking quietly, Barbara grew tired. We went into the bedroom, closing the door behind us. I sat beside her as she removed the new silk shirt and satin pants, pulled her cotton t-shirt over her lacy camisole, and climbed under the covers. Smiling up at me, she said, "Today was the happiest day of my life." Then she closed her eyes and slept.

Barbara
February 4

The last month has been a whirlwind. First Dr. Grant's call telling me that my LDH enzyme level was elevated, then an abdominal CAT scan that showed liver metastases, an ultrasound test that ruled out kidney involvement, a second opinion recommending an experimental procedure, our bonding ceremony, my hospitalization for a liver infusion, recuperation at home with a visit from Gail, then one from Stan.

There is no point in keeping up with time. My life happens too fast for reflection. I am too anxious to write. There are too many people. There is too much interaction. Mainly the aloneness it takes to write a journal entry is often unbearable for me.

I am very afraid of further metastases, that even as I write the cancer spreads. The uncertainty of this disease is shaped now by my fear, my most pessimistic projections. All this going on inside my body and yet I don't feel anything. I'm not sick. I'm not in pain, but mysterious and lethal processes may be invading my body and not only can I not control any of it, I don't even know what's going on. It takes a CAT scan—and how I hate those now—to peer inside, to make visible those altered, strangely shaped cells, those colonies called tumors. I must wait for the next CAT scan on February 17 to see if the liver infusion was successful.

Sandy
February 6

The liver infusion was a nightmare. This was the first time

Barbara has been in such pain. I lay beside her at night, poised on my cot, peering through the bars of her hospital bed, watching her sleep, being sure she received her pain medication on time, holding her hand.

I needed to see how relaxed or pained her face was at every moment. To hear her voice: how strained, calm, or sleepy her tone. To read her stories as she relaxed into occasional naps. To monitor the I.V. fluids. To help her to the bathroom. To infuse her heart with my love.

Each evening at five, a different friend met me in the hospital lobby, took me to dinner, drove me home while I showered and packed fresh clothes, then returned me to the hospital. I don't remember the dinners, what we said, what I ate. Time was suspended whenever I was away from her. I raced through our empty rooms, gathering mail, writing down phone messages, calls that I would return from a phone in the hospital corridor while Barbara slept. "You need to get away for a few hours," my friends would gently admonish me. I didn't understand why.

My home was now in room 502 of Moffit Hospital, where Barbara was receiving chemo-embolization. On her yellow pad are the questions and description of the "procedure"—that bloodless medical word. "Come into hospital," she has written. "Catheter put in groin, similar to angiogram. Check to see if the portals are open and, if so, a shot combined in a gel or collagen is infused into the liver, which holds it there for a few days. From there," her notes continue, "up to the ward for I.V. fluids for two or three days. Pain meds for nausea and fever." The fever kills cancer cells, we were told. It's the best option, we were assured.

But even in those hushed and melancholy rooms, we laughed together. This is what saved us from despair. As it has so many times before.

On the last night, Barbara awakened complaining of pains in her chest. The technicians bustled in with a forbidding piece of machinery, brusquely telling me they needed to take an x-ray and I had to stand outside the door. I climbed out of my cot, frightened, and padded out into the hall. When they were finished, the pain turned out to be "nothing," and they ordered more meds. "Go back to sleep," they instructed. As if she could.

Only after they left the room and I had tiptoed back, did Barbara look at me. "You were out in the hall like that?" she said, her face breaking into a wide grin. For the first time, I noticed I was wearing a blue t-shirt that announced in bold letters, *Take Back The Night. Bemidji, MN. 1985.* No other clothes. Just me, naked in the hallway wearing a blue t-shirt. We collapsed in exhausted hysteria at the unexpected and ridiculous sight I had provided for the night staff. Leaning over her bed to kiss her good night, I whispered, "We're going home in the morning. I have an entire wardrobe of hospital hallway ensembles. I'll model them all for you."

Barbara
February 12

Now the two of us are in Hawaii, quiet at last. Sandy is calm and happy here and looks better than she has in the last two years. I'm relaxed, but continue to be catapulted into a thousand oscillating feelings, a hundred rises and falls of tears, laughter, joy, pleasure, pain, panic. It is becoming harder and harder to be me—the unreliable body, the unpredictable energy, the surges and sags of emotion.

I think of Kathy Grant, my doctor, with an appreciation of her sardonic humor, with gratitude and with love. She opened my eyes to something new, the study of palms. For the last two years, I have enjoyed learning about the many varieties of the species, in Australia as well as here. How I wish she could save my life.

I am angry sometimes because I see that the best of Sandy is yet to come and I will not have it. I hate the idea someone else will get it. But that's life and death and life. I have had the best of who Sandy is now and she has had the best of me, and here we are in Hawaii. Sandy is on the porch reading and there is now a quiet serenity to both of us; indeed it is a lovely pleasure, a sweet comfort.

ESSENCES

FEBRUARY – MARCH 1987

Sandy
February 16

Barbara astonishes me with her lifelong passion, now intensified, to leap into new ideas, immerse herself in new bodies of information. Since our return from Hawaii, she has begun to read about Bolivian fabrics, medieval manuscripts, coral reefs, and book restoration. Each fires her enthusiasm and she becomes animated, eager to talk about this new subject, to teach me what she is learning. We manage now to have a brief adventure every day. A movie. A walk through an art gallery. A rich meal. Our week in Hawaii sustained and nourished me, steadied me for what will come next, for whatever is required.

Barbara
February 16

I am sitting in the hospital with Sandy, waiting for the CAT scan results, waiting to see how effective the liver infusion procedure was. To see if the cancer has moved into other internal organs. An hour ago I took a chest x-ray to see if it has spread into my lungs.

I'm a wreck. I've got a headache, tight muscles in my neck, and I'm nauseous. And these are just today's effects. I've had incessant swallowing for the last two weeks, a cough, and difficulty breathing for the last week. All this is completely mysterious to me. Is it a symptom of lung metastases or is it psychologically based? If it's psychosomatic this will convince me that the mind is the strongest organ of all.

What would be a good report? No evidence of further spread. A fifty percent reduction of liver tumors. That they can do the procedure again in four to six months after monitoring me. That my blood levels come as close to normal as possible. A bad report would indicate spread, not much reduction, and that the procedure did not help.

LATER THAT SAME DAY: The report showed a reduction in the liver but a spread to the lungs. While they were looking in one direction, the cancer spread in another.

Barbara's letter to friends
February 20

Dear Friends,

I have some more bad news. While the cancer was being stabilized by local treatment to the liver, it systemically spread to my lungs. This cancer is an aggressive son-of-a-bitch and now I must be on systemic chemotherapy the rest of my life to keep it under control.

Given the rate of diffusion of this disease and because it spread to my lungs within six weeks of the liver metastasis, I thought I'd only have a few months to live. I have an extremely aggressive cell which nearly doubles every twenty days. But my doctor is hopeful about the effects of chemotherapy on these metastases and thinks I might have six months, at the low end, to possibly fifteen months at the high end. I am grateful for this. Thank God for such things.

Again I am ready and know that I have the physical and mental stamina to go the distance. I know that your hearts are with me and I feel your love and support in this yet again difficult fight.

I hate the thought of being on heavy chemo again, but it's the only thing that will stop the further invasion of my body. I've already written to you about the side effects, but I have to do it to stay alive, so there's no point in making this debatable or a question of preference. At least not now.

I am frightened occasionally but I've decided to face the future with as much help as I can from drugs, ranging from anti-nauseants to tranquilizers and sleeping pills. Anything that can make me more comfortable, I'm open to taking. If my body can't hold out or the pain is unbearable, I'll recalculate my choices at that time and take whatever medication is appropriate.

One thing that makes me feel intensely alive is to keep on learning, to be on that exciting edge of new subject matter, in effect, of a new world to know. The other day I went to my first antiquarian book fair and had a great time. I loved learning about the old books, loved their thick-papered textures. I had the occasion to reflect upon the history of the technology of printing, the use of images, literacy, the new Center for the Book at the Library of Congress. Using my brain, keeping interests vital, and learning new things all contribute to a deep sense of aliveness.

Another process is happening to me as well, one that probably has a name, but it eludes me. It has to do with coming to an inner essentialism. After loving so many styles, forms, composers, and periods in music, I can now say with certainty that Bach is my favorite. And this same process is going on in other areas too. I'm now able to say my favorite poet is Gerard Manley Hopkins, for the density and musicality of the language. I'm now able to say all the things that are essential to my taste: spareness, appreciation of the architecture, the ability to make structure part of the aesthetic. The purity of line, the elegance of geometry.

I seem to be getting simpler and simpler to myself, seem to know very clearly what my essence is. Things aren't so complicated anymore. I can even pick my favorite color and favorite ethnic food. I experience my choices and preferences as a step towards clarity, rather than limitation. Simplification, maybe that's what this process is called. It feels more like coming into one's fullest and truest self and simply acknowledging what is. The self revealed to the self, observed by the self. Simply. Coming to the essentials.

I am also aware of coming into a new openness, a lightness, an ease with which I face the completion of my life. I have known ecstasy and despair. I have lived well and richly and have a well-loved life. I love many people and am loved by them. I am fully present, fully conscious, and fully human, as much as anyone who has ever explored the dimensions of what it means to be human.

Life trembles with vibrations of living. The world is totally charged with, as Gerard Manley Hopkins puts it, "the grandeur of God." I watch things come into themselves, moments being born, things revealing their essences, things in transition. All things seem infused with a life force, a vitality. Life throbs and quivers with its aliveness. Life is mysterious, full, moving in a slowly forward motion like an oceanic wave, with its deep currents unseen.

Although Heidegger is not my favorite philosopher, there are now lessons to be learned from him. A dog dogs. The world worlds. Barbara Barbaras. A world where nouns and verbs dissolve into essences. Barbara is still Barbara-ing and that makes me feel alive in yet another way.

I am trying to make sense of this to myself and to you, to make intelligible to you the path that you will create for yourself, when it is your time.

With love,

Barbara

Sandy
February 22

It is two years since the diagnosis. We continue.

Yesterday Barbara was too weak to manage even a short walk around the block. She tries so hard to be "cheerful," to make what is possible into what is fun. But yesterday she could not walk past the cleaners or the coffee shop, could not call hello to the neighbors and shopkeepers she has known for fifteen years. Even knowing this weakness is temporary, a result of the omnipresent chemo, she felt overwhelmed. Her face crumpled and she began to cry about every-thing she would no longer see. All the adventures we would no longer have together. I wrapped my arms around her as she sobbed and unexpectedly I, too, began to weep. Both of us were simply exhausted from the weeks and months of talk, of searching for the words that would connect us in this nightmare. Silently we climbed into bed and huddled together. There were no words now, just as there were no words then—two years ago when she got the diagnosis. Just our bodies pressed closely together, our arms wrapped tightly around each other, the sound of grief—hers and mine.

I awoke this morning feeling gratitude. I thought about all the people who lose loved ones to a car crash, a heart attack, a stroke. Without any advance warning, the person they care most about is simply gone. Barbara and I are engaged in a process of leave-taking that is excruciatingly painful, but it is also conscious and truthful. When she dies, I will have had an experience that both prepared and cushioned me. For that I am grateful. And I also know I couldn't have understood that without being held in Barbara's arms as I wept.

Barbara
February 28

The problem: when I have sensations in my body, it's an unshar-able experience; I become aware of the limitations of language in describing those sensations and thus relieving myself of their burden. I grow increasingly aware of the illusion of the intersubjective nature of the world. The world is shattered, language dissolves, and there is only body and its feeling. Even a private language, such as I have with Sandy, is a self-contradiction. There cannot be private language. Interactions slow down, collapse, lose their meaning and integrity. I observe myself trying to talk but am isolated in an imprisoned, solipsistic world, experiencing the terror, panic, and isolation be-cause we believe in common language, common culture, common understandings.

I believed I could know Sandy and her mind, and so create the warmth of being connected. Our knowledge of each other is, by now, taken for granted. But it is the intrusion of the body sensation that

makes loneliness unbearable. Yet to bear this is part of my human-
ness and makes me part of our connected human condition.

Sandy
March 5

Barbara and I went to a Stephen Levine seminar. We had
attended a weekend workshop last year that was moving and useful to
us both. I was eager to return and urged Barbara (who was more hesi-
tant) to join me, feeling that, after such bad news, we would be
strengthed by his calm, knowledgeable approach to loss and to death.

After an hour of listening to people speak, of feeling the room fill
with the sounds of grief, Barbara impatiently turned to me and
whispered, "There are a lot of tormented people here, aren't there?"

"Yes," I said. "There sure seem to be."

She listened for a while longer, then asked, "Have you come to
terms with my death?"

"Yes," I replied, startled at the question but quite certain about
my answer. "Yes, I have."

She pushed herself heavily to her feet. "Me too. Let's go then.
We have no more work to do here."

We left and walked out onto the Marina, entering a bright, clear,
sun-filled day. After a short walk, we ate barbecued ribs and ice
cream, then went to the movies. "As long as I have life, we might as
well enjoy it instead of agonizing about the fact that it will end.
Right?"

I took her hand and held on. "Right," I assured us both. "Let's
live the life we have."

Barbara
March 7

Last night I dreamed that our dog, Sembei, was hurt in an accident. Sandy and I were fighting and she threw a champagne glass
onto the floor. It shattered and Sembei's foot got a big sliver of glass
stuck in it. Interpretation: my attempt to understand the shock, hurt,
pain of my mastectomy and preparation now for surgery in two weeks
to place a Port-A-Cath near where my breast once was. Also my

awareness of Sandy's rage. It was a choice I made—to be with her instead of others, people less angry, sweeter. But something in me was attracted to Sandy, despite her rage. I think it's the intensity of her devotion and passion.

Sandy
March 8

The house has been full this month. Both Janaea and Alison came for a visit, then two of Barbara's colleagues from Vermont College stayed with us on their way to a colloquium. Barbara is too fragile to accompany them and feels the loss of engagement with an intellectual community very acutely these days. After they left, Deborah, a woman she has known since graduate school, arrived; then Peter, a friend for nearly thirty years, flew in from New York. A satisfying but emotionally overwhelming time for her.

I am trying to be responsive, supportive, careful, and attentive. I exhaust myself with the effort. Barbara has been pulling away a bit, partly as a result of the overstimulation from all the company and partly as a way to deal with her own feelings. I get terrified when this happens and all the abandonment, loneliness, and isolation that has trailed me all my life resurfaces.

Last week I went for my weekly therapy appointment with Myra and told her how hard I was working and how invisible and misunderstood I was feeling. After I finished talking, Myra gently remonstrated, "You know, it's important for you not to use your hurt feelings as a way to create distance and protection from the experience of Barbara's dying."

She is right, of course. If I am to be present, then it means being able to tolerate Barbara's pain, rage, disappointment, resentment, as well as all the deepening closeness and sustenance we provide each other. I have come to the sad recognition that not everything will ever be resolved or worked through. Being open to each moment is all there is. Allowing love to exist without judgment or expectation. That is my lesson now.

Barbara
March 11

My sister, Ruth, has come to visit and brought along Asher, my eleven-month-old nephew, who has the sunniest disposition I ever saw. With Asher, I laugh. With Ruth, I cry. We talked about what it was like for her to have me as an older sister and wept together for the love and closeness between us. During her visit Sandy and I had a healing circle of sixteen close friends who were asked to bring poetry and prose to read: selections that addressed themes of courage, strength, and endurance. Some did not read but talked, instead, about how their experience of their own lives has changed as they confront my eventual death. To me this is human chemo-therapy, just like a shot in the arm. I need to know that I can provide others a way to approach the ultimate, inescapable experience we all must face. That other people can learn from this and make their lives fuller and richer—and more real—is extremely gratifying to me.

Sandy
March 16

All the visitors are gone and the house is empty, quiet, and ours again. This morning, before I left for the office, Barbara and I jitter-bugged to 1940s big-band music. When we dance in the morning, I remember the old Barbara and Sandy. The way things used to be.

Barbara
March 20

It is 3:30 a.m., and I am again battling nausea and vomiting. This time from the use of only one single agent, Adriamycin. Two years ago, when on FAC (5-FU, Adriamycin and Cytoxan), also a horribly nausea-producing combination, I used to stay in bed with Sandy and run to the bathroom to vomit all day and all night. We would watch movies on the new VCR, bought deliberately for the purpose of providing entertainment for a mind that could not concentrate on reading and a body too exhausted to do anything but watch a screen and doze off intermittently. Sometimes I would vomit twenty-five times within the first two days. Even if it had only been a flu that caused such convulsive eruptions, I still would have been exhausted for two days following the vomiting.

But now I take Prednisone, a strong anti-inflammatory agent, which has somewhat decreased the nausea and vomiting. True, waves of nausea come, but I am more likely to have dry heaves. I kneel and stare into the toilet, but I don't always fill the bowl with the contents of my stomach.

My nights are often interrupted by sleeplessness and I usually take a tranquilizer or sleeping pill because of the anxiety and fast heartbeat, the incessant swallowing, the physical signs of nervousness. It has been worse lately because I now experience symptoms in my body: coughing and knocking sounds from my lungs. The doctor said I may have a pleural rub, where the lining of the lungs is filled with fluid and creaks against the chest wall.

The first night it happened, twelve days ago, my body involuntarily began to shiver with fear and I needed to take a strong dose of sleeping medication. Sandy reported the next morning she hadn't slept a wink all night. She had been listening to my breathing, attentive, on watch, making sure I stayed alive.

When the cancer was only in my liver, I was assured that death would be fairly painless, accompanied by diminished body function and an accumulation of fluids throughout my body. But now that the cancer has spread to my lungs, I am very frightened that I will suffer with air clogged in my throat and chest.

How vulnerable the throat is. Not even a functioning part of the breathing system but merely a mechanical conduit for air into the lungs. The trachea resides in the throat and is experienced as the seat of breathing. Witness the hand clutching the throat when breathing fails. The hand doesn't clutch the nostrils, where the air enters, or the lungs, where it is transformed, but the throat, where it goes into the body's internal system for the oxygen/carbon dioxide exchange. The nose passage is merely the entrance to the freeway. The throat is where you get on.

I am afraid of not breathing well but have again been reassured that lung disease is not painful and that I really won't have a problem catching my breath. And there will be medication to kill the pain. Medication to help breathing. Medication to dull the terror.

Barbara
March 25

The noise in my lungs has disappeared and Dr. Grant thinks it's probably a healing reaction and that the pleural lining is not necessarily filled with malignant fluid. What a relief! I fell asleep easily and gently, enormously relieved that the symptom which appeared just weeks ago is almost done and that it didn't mean my death. It didn't kill me.

Barbara
March 28

Friday night. The end of a very hard week. Back into the hospital, more anesthesia and surgery. This time to insert a Port-A-Cath into my chest, to create an opening in my body where the chemotherapy can enter. The staples hurt and I am again vomiting from the chemotherapy dripping slowly into me. My arm and shoulder muscles are in spasm. I feel both inconsolably sad and like a wounded soldier. I remember Deena's line in *Tree*, in which she describes her experience with breast cancer. "This wound is a political wound. I am a political prisoner. I am a soldier wounded in a war you didn't know we were fighting . . . but a soldier should not be ashamed that a bullet has struck her."

I think about the ritual we held this month. About how many people have told me how much they admire my courage in the face of death. But courage in the face of life is much more important and much more dangerous.

BEARING WITNESS

Sandy

It's April, 1987. Our forty-fourth and forty-ninth birthdays are approaching—the last we would spend together.

We are preparing to fly to New York, both of us tense with expectation. I am wary of land mines awaiting even the slightest stumble. Barbara is guarded and cautious about alarming her parents. We have prepared well, counseled by both friends and therapists. "We," they all say, need to stay steady and connected in the anticipated maelstrom of family pressure, fear, insecurity, and demands. "We" will try.

Barbara's birthday is celebrated the day after we arrive. She looks beautiful in a purple silk shirt, awkward in the wig her mother insists that she wear. Her parents' Coney Island apartment is filled with her sister, brother-in-law, nephew, and the enthusiastic and concentrated attention of elderly Jews eating lobster, an extravagant treat. Instructions are freely offered, the familiar sucking of bones now transposed to claws, the urgings of "Eat. Eat."

Later there is a chocolate cake and everyone sings "Happy Birthday." Barbara's eyes meet her mother's, both filled with tears.

Mother and daughter silently rub them away with the backs of their hands and sit down to cake, fruit salad, and loving.

The love here. There is no bottom to this river of love. It draws me in, bathes, and softens me. Food, sleep, comfort, warmth—all the basic human needs are checked, rechecked, and, temporarily, they are satisfied.

"Yes, we slept well. Yes, we were warm enough. Yes, the lox was excellent. No, I don't want another pillow or potato. Yes, I am glad to go to the store. No, it won't tire me out." Basic. All of it so basic. Feelings too. Sad, happy, excited, depressed. The emotional world of primary colors. These kind, bewildered people have brought me into their family. I have entered, filled with my own loneliness, my own grief.

In a few days we will go to Ruth and Marc's for the Passover *seder* and I fear the excess. Too much chopped liver, too much enthusiasm, too many pictures, too much attention—everyone teetering on the dangerous edge of Barbara's cancer, Barbara's sharply etched baldness, Barbara's fatigue. I anticipate that I will smile until my face feels stretched garishly, straining upward. That I will talk and talk, and eat too much, and eagerly help clean up, and relievedly draw apart.

But this does not happen. Barbara interrupted the formal *seder* ceremony with a passionate impromptu talk about the Warsaw Ghetto, about oppression, about our responsibilities as Jews. We took turns reading from the *Hagaddah*, with Barbara's father reading the prayers in Hebrew and her mother skipping her turn discreetly, her inability to read, her inability to see, gently overlooked.

And finally after the dinner, the lighting of the candles, the prayers, the remembrances. Someone put folk music on the phonograph. I no longer remember who began, but soon Barbara, her mother, sister, and father were in a spinning circle, laughing, stomping their feet. The circle closing. Dancing. Moving.

Barbara

It is a beautiful spring Sunday in New York. Sandy and I spent the night in a friend's apartment at NYU housing. We have been told to try Elephant Castle for breakfast. We have a few plans for today and then a big, gorgeous, expensive dinner in Manhattan. It's Sandy's forty-ninth birthday and I've promised her a perfect day in Manhattan. Spring and all.

Down West Broadway to Prince, right on Prince to get eggs and coffee, good toast and jam. Almost noon, almost time for a very special event. The forty-fourth commemoration of the Uprising of the Warsaw Ghetto will be held at Public School 41. I was born April 9, 1943, ten days before the Uprising. Sandy was born April 19, 1938, five years before but on the same date.

I had always wanted to attend but was too scared. My parents went every year since I can remember and would return at the end of the day as ghostlike as those they had gone to mourn. They were bereft, inconsolable. April 19 was always like that.

Now that I am terribly sick and never know when I can go anywhere again, I've decided it is time to go to the memorial celebration of the forty-fourth anniversary. This is one event I don't want to live or die without experiencing.

We turn the corner and abruptly leave the world of the *New York Times*, cappuccinos, and crooked Village streets. In contrast to Yuppie Soho at breakfast time, we see old Jews headed for P.S. 41. Short, grey, aged, dressed in polyester and sensible, low shoes, solemnly attired for this occasion. They stand at the door, waiting for friends to arrive.

We enter, pay a dollar admission, and go into the school auditorium filled with photo blow-ups of those who died, their names written in Yiddish.

Sandy

MY FORTY-NINTH BIRTHDAY. We awoke on a high, narrow bed in a Washington Square Park apartment, the generosity of a friend who was spending the weekend with her lover in Brooklyn. We arrived late the night before, Barbara having attended a concert with Peter, and I having had dinner with Janaea, readying herself emotionally for her thirtieth birthday. Each of our evenings was intensely satisfying, emotionally exhilarating, and very private. We met at the apartment late that night with little talk, just the continuing pleasure of coming together after having been apart for a few hours.

I awaken on this, the morning of my forty-ninth birthday and think about attending a memorial service for the survivors of the Holocaust. I lie beside Barbara as she sleeps, remembering my return to college at thirty-five and that year of study, its focus an effort to retrace a history blurred by my parents' efforts at assimilation.

I was raised with little sense of Jewish history beyond that of gray-bearded patriarchs, an occasional Queen Esther on *Purim*, and prayers that were memorized, never understood or questioned. I was confirmed at thirteen and, like the majority of my class, stopped attending temple except for the social demands of the High Holy Days.

My college thesis on the Holocaust had its genesis in a history I saw surface in the Black community of the '60s and '70s. Those Black young women and men sought to trace their pasts, struggled to understand the roots of their experience, and ultimately exploded into an advocacy, a pride, and a passion that was both unfamiliar and exhilarating to me. I, too, needed to study, to enter the past beyond the carefully manicured lives of my parents and their contemporaries and beyond the carefully screened remembrances of my grandparents.

I read for months. History, economics, journals, political analysis, everything I could find. I immersed myself, listening to the words of the survivors, analyzing the political currents that led to the annihilation of millions, beginning to understand the ways the lives that came before ours inform and alter our own ethical and moral choices.

Barbara grew up in an immigrant family whose daily lives were witness. Their suffering and fundamental grief robbed her of the chance for a sense of safety, the possibility of joy, and the ability to have an unencumbered childhood.

Each year her parents and their friends went to memorial services for those who perished in the Warsaw Ghetto Uprising. She remembers them returning home, pale, silent, drained. Their going, their bearing witness, was an unquestioned dimension of their lives. Barbara never joined them, needing to protect herself from this excess, this demanding sadness, this bleak landscape upon which her mother and father lived.

But on this morning, we awoke preparing to attend a memorial

service to honor those who fought back. It was an inevitable consequence of the direction of our joining a gay and lesbian synagogue
and our ceremony of commitment. Our new relationship to Judaism.
We walked through the Village streets of lower New York, telling
stories of our younger selves who had inhabited those same streets
decades before. Arm in arm, we walked, recounting stories of early-
adolescent bohemian adventures. She showed me the first nightclub
she ever went to, for which she had put on earrings and makeup as
she rode the subway from Brooklyn. I described the years just after
my divorce, alone with two young children. We talked and pointed at
buildings, towards shops, at cafes that were once dry cleaners or
drugstores. We gave the stories of our earlier lives substance and form
on the streets on which they had been lived. We walked and walked
the streets of the Village and after nearly an hour, turned the corner
to West Eleventh Street. We passed the apartment house I had lived
in after my divorce, the market that awaited me each day at five-
fifteen, the lines long with weary mothers. The memorial service was
being held at P.S. 41, the school that both of my children had
attended.

We entered the building with the others. All of them old. Small.
Walking slowly, talking in low voices. We passed through the double
doors and memories engulfed me. The hallway, the lunchroom, the
water fountain, the pale green walls, the principal's office. I remembered Janaea, with whom I had had dinner less that twelve hours
before, in second grade, starring as Wendy in *Peter Pan*, in the
auditorium, the same one we were now entering. The stage now
filled with placards of the fallen martyrs of the Warsaw Ghetto. The
auditorium slowly filled with old Jews who had come, along with the
two of us, to bear witness.

At the front of the auditorium, just below the stage was a semi-
circle of the thirty men and women who formed the chorus. The
women wore starched, white blouses, long, floor-length, black skirts,
with orthopedic shoes peeking out beneath their carefully pressed
hems. They sat, arranged on brown folding chairs holding sheet
music in their laps. We made our way to our seats and settled into
them, busying ourselves folding our coats, arranging ourselves, while
observing the women and men who were gathering.

At exactly 1 p.m., the chorus began to sing with pride, strength, slightly wavering voices, and much passion. The music was unfamiliar to me. Barbara leaned over and whispered, "'Mountain of Shoes.' That's the name of the song. 'Mountain of Shoes.'" The song, all the songs, were in Yiddish, for that was the language of witness. The entire service, speakers, poets, music, was in Yiddish. This was the language to describe, evoke, and capture the feelings of the participants, the lives of the dead. I sat beside Barbara, unable to fully enter, the Yiddish a scrim between me and the others. Not a thick barrier, but a gauzy, transparent separation. I was able finally to surrender to the sound that washed over me, for Yiddish is an expressive language, but I could not understand what was being said. I looked over and saw Barbara intent, unmoving, inside each moment. I envied her. Even with the price she had paid: the daily, relentless pain of her parents' lives, the racing away and inching back to her legacy of Jewishness, the loss. I wanted to be enveloped by these men and women, these Jews. I, too, wanted to be a part of this continuum, this bearing witness to the fallen martyrs. I wanted to belong to this moment, but could not understand what was being said.

I reached over and took Barbara's hand, this peasant hand, this hand that has gentled me, this hand that has filled my body with love and with pleasure, this hand that has stroked and comforted me through so many nights, so many days. I sat listening to the soothing, familiar, indecipherable sounds of Yiddish and began to cry. Letting the tears slide down my face, curl into my mouth. But when I looked around I saw that I was the only one crying, for these old people had cried for years, for decades. They had cried themselves to emptiness. And still they came, for their presence was required. Not to mourn any longer, for the mourning had ended and yet could never end. It began to feel presumptuous to cry. Crying was too easy. There was something more complicated going on here in the stolid bodies and unflinching faces of these old Jews. Something I did not yet understand. It seemed impertinent to imagine an understanding that would envelop such suffering, such loss.

Barbara would die, probably within the year. We both knew that. Her cancer was too advanced for us to pretend otherwise. I was preparing to experience what would be the most profound loss of my nearly fifty years. Life without her was unimaginable, barren, terrifying. And yet her mother will lose her first-born child. I try to think about Janaea dying and I cannot even allow my thoughts to trace such an image on my mind's eye. Bad luck to even think such a thought. But all these people in this small grammar school auditorium had lost children, husbands, wives, parents, friends, aunts, neighbors. And they had continued. Perhaps simply enduring is the way to bear witness.

We left the building, blinking as the bright sunshine of a sunny Village day filled our eyes. Walking to the corner, the sounds and the images of the afternoon receding before the onrush of taxis, buses, people, urgency, Barbara asked me where I wanted to go. She reminded me gently it was my birthday and I could spend the day doing whatever I wanted. Suddenly, I felt depleted, exhausted. I couldn't find a way to shift gears, a way past the sounds, the faces, the music. I couldn't imagine a museum, an art gallery, an excellent meal, a cafe that would create a transitional moment. I didn't want a transitional moment. I wanted to return to Coney Island, to an apartment where her parents, too frail now to have accompanied us into Manhattan, waited. They went to a local memorial service the night before and hoped, without asking, that we would return and want to eat. Food, the expression of love. They tell stories of never having enough food to eat. Of feeling grateful to have hot and cold running water indoors. Of a sense of enoughness. So now they make stewed prunes. A potato *kugel. Tsimmes.* Boiled brisket. Food I never ate as a child and rarely as an adult. Food that I eat daily when we are visiting here. Food that fills me, warms me, connects me. I want to go back to Coney Island and eat. I told Barbara this and she nodded her head at once. Of course. Of course.

Doing Laps

April – August 1987

Barbara
April 22

I am in a state of anguish about having to leave New York and about separating from my mother and my sister. About the inconsolable nature of my grief, the nature and pain of my illness, which is relentless, and my unbelievable need for Sandy, which is almost overwhelming.

The words "I am dying" hum through my head endlessly and without relief. I hear that melody all the time. It is the beginning of me humming a lullaby to myself. What can I write about this aloneness? If you think standing by yourself waiting for someone to talk to you is lonely, if you think holidays alone are lonely, if you think that not having a relationship for a long time is lonely, if you think that the long, frightening nights after a divorce are lonely—you cannot know the aloneness of one who faces death, looking it squarely in the eye.

Love is so complicated, so hard for me now. I who never knew I needed much, who never let too many needs surface, who took care of so many other people. I who never asked for very much; I who was alone for so long; I who now have a real partner; I have never felt so needy in my life.

So desperate, so clinging, so frightened. Alone. Alone. By myself. I'll go my way by myself. I wish somebody would come inside and cradle my heart.

Sandy
May 5

Barbara is on different chemo now and needs to spend three of every twenty-eight days in the hospital. She gets an injection of Adriamycin, a bolus of Mitomycin, then a slow infusion with Vinblastine. The process is very toxic and requires monitoring. While there is very little pain, Barbara is like a prisoner attached to tubes and bottles.

She lies in bed drawing the computer-face of the machine that inexorably dispenses the chemotherapy into her Port-A-Cath. Counting, watching, waiting for the numbers to climb to 1066, when the process will be complete. In her journal she scrawls, "874 and counting up. Perhaps food will come soon. Food as distraction." She adds columns of numbers to determine, to the second, how many more interminable minutes before the pump beside her will be emptied, before she can be unhooked from the tubes and machinery, before we can go home. Conversation is nearly impossible now. We sit and watch the numbers passing, moving higher, the I.V. bag slowly collapsing, the only sound that of the ticking as the liquids are released into her body.

But, even here, Barbara has created a goal to be accomplished each day, time too precious to be wasted. Now, in this sterile place, we do "laps."

Each morning at seven-thirty, like the clockwork of her computer-driven chemotherapy dispenser, I arrive at the hospital with a thermos of French roast coffee and the New York Times. She doesn't read the Times—her concern for the wars outside her body is limited now—but the ritual requires both coffee and the Times. She is usually asleep when I enter the room, and hearing me, even before opening her eyes, she smiles. She reaches her arms out as I lean over the bed and embrace her, still soft from sleep. I sit beside her asking her how she slept as I crank up the bed. She sips the coffee and glances briefly at the front page of the paper.

Then she announces, "Today we'll do twelve laps. Three before breakfast, three before lunch, three more if I have a visitor in the afternoon, and three after dinner." These laps, athletic though they may sound, describe our painstaking walk up and down the hospital corridor.

She swings her swollen legs over the side of the bed, careful not to entangle them with the tubes that emerge from her chest and connect to the I.V. stand. She slides the machinery towards the bathroom, to wash, to ready herself for another day. I carefully drape the red terry cloth bathrobe (the one I bought her for our sixth anniversary so many years ago) around her, around the Port-A-Cath, as she slips into her green, European loafers.

As we wheel out into the hall, Barbara insists upon pushing the I.V. stand herself and bends forward to keep balance. I whisper to her to try to stand up straight, worried about her chronic, lower back pain, and she remembers, smiles encouragingly at me, stands ramrod straight, one hand on the I.V. stand, the other tucked into mine. Together we glide off to begin the daily laps.

By now we know most of the patients and staff who walk through the corridors. Staff nod, greet us by name as they stride briskly by, their heels making purposeful taps on the tile floor. Most other patients shuffle past, keeping their eyes and faces averted. Barbara remains oblivious to most of this hallway interaction—sliding the I.V. stand along and remembering to stand up straight takes her full attention. She is totally focused on getting to the end of the corridor and back three times before her energy begins to fade.

The first time we did laps together, I tried to make conversation, to help me pretend that this was only Sandy and Barbara taking a walk. I talked about food. Asked her if she wanted poached sole from a nearby cafe for lunch. Or perhaps Greek salad? A dozen oysters? Maybe bran and raisin muffins? Gelato? Anything to augment the bland hospital food, to whet her well-developed taste buds.

Finally, with growing impatience, she said firmly, "Sandy, I'm in the hospital and eating good food isn't going to make any of this easier. There is no point in pretending I'm any place else. While I'm here, I'll be here. After I'm discharged we can go someplace for dinner." After that admonition I never knew quite what to say on our laps, so remained silent and intent on helping her accomplish the goal she had set for that day. One day we walked to the obstetric unit so Barbara could learn something about premature babies. She talked to the nurses, peered solemnly at the infants with electrodes on their vulnerable chests, as she balanced precariously beside her own I.V. stand.

Some mornings when I arrived, she declared the number of laps we had walked the previous day was sufficient but that we now needed to time them and see if we couldn't do them faster. A bit of hospital aerobics—good for the spirit, if not the heart. Each day that she accomplished her goal, however small, was an affirmation of her courage, her life. Her basic sense of possibility and optimism prevailed. No day was wasted, without purpose, even if it was only to "do laps" hunched over an I.V. stand, wrapped in a red terry cloth bathrobe with a ceramic clown pin on the lapel, wearing her green loafers, a painful reminder of a happier time.

Sandy
May 8

Barbara returned home from this last hospital stay and announced, "Now that this is over, and I don't have to be back for twenty-eight days, let's take a trip. I want to get away from cancer for a little while. Let's call Stan and go someplace, just the three of us. Somewhere warm, where there are wonderful museums, history, rich food." Almost at once we decided on Florence, a city Barbara had always wanted to see. I made the preparations. Three days after Barbara was released from the hospital, we were packed and on a plane to Italy.

Sandy
May 1987

FLORENCE DIARY. Stan, Barbara, and I arrived in Florence after a grueling trip, damp with exhaustion, tension, and excitement. We race from Santa Croce to the Uffizi, dotting our excursions with cappuccino and pasta. The architecture, frescoes, churches, and museums are rich with the details of life during the early- and mid-Renaissance. Barbara is greedy, eager for everything: the art, the food, the history. There is a desperate sense of urgency. So much to see. So much to learn.

The fourth day we walked through the mausoleums, crypts, and statuary in the cemetery of San Miniato. We sat on a bench surrounded with tombstones, beside a life-sized statue of a man in a World War II uniform waltzing with his young bride, a moment of youthful happiness captured forever in stone. Barbara asked me for the first time how I would choose to be buried if I knew my death was approaching. Haltingly I told her that I wanted to be cremated, to quicken my body's natural return to the earth. She spoke then of her ambivalence about a traditional Jewish burial, her uncertainty about where she would be buried, how her parents would feel about cremation — the first indication that she has begun to think about the possibility of dying before them. I assured her that I would support her in whatever decision she made, whether to be buried alongside her parents in their plot on Coney Island or in a cemetery in San Francisco, or whether to be cremated with her ashes scattered in the garden.

"My place is in the garden," she murmured. "It is the one spot in the world I feel I belong. The place where I have tended, nurtured, and created life."

I reminded her of the many books and articles dedicated to her, the outpourings of moving and generous letters from friends and colleagues. The work she is doing. The work we do together. So many lives have been touched. And some even altered. She has already brought forth a multitude.

She listened quietly, then said, "I think I need to talk about these issues with Rabbi Kahn. I'll call him when we return home." Then she rose, signaling the end of our conversation, and we began the walk back to the hotel.

The next day Barbara collapsed from exhaustion. We had left our hotel at dawn to watch the city awaken. Before long I realized that, inadvertently, we had gone too far. It was still very early and the taxis were not yet out on the narrow cobblestone streets. Barbara barely managed to stumble back to the hotel, needing to rest at every corner. She slept for most of the remainder of the day, awakening again near midnight. As we lay in each other's arms, she talked about her fear and her sense of missed opportunities. "So many things I wanted to do with you. So many places to go. So much life to share," she whimpered, holding onto me. I, too, wept until, exhausted, we both fell back into a restless sleep. She dreamed she was dying and wanted to be buried in Santa Croce next to Michelangelo. For the first time, I, too, dreamed of my life after her death. Unfamiliar people tried to introduce me to other women and I, outraged, yelled at them, "I already have a partner and don't want another one."

When we both awoke the next morning, fresh from our dreams, we understood we had moved imperceptibly closer to the inevitability of this ending, her death.

Two days later she awoke to find her left arm nearly twice as large as her right one. She knew immediately that it was a new symptom and we both grew frightened. Stan and I arranged for us all to return to the United States at once.

Barbara
May 31

There has been a change in my medical status. Cancer is growing again in my liver. The symptoms are pretty terrible. I have more fatigue than ever before. A profound loss of energy and direction and an inability to be "present." I'm more detached, perhaps saying my good-byes, in a way. I am just doing what is necessary to survive. My mind and body are doing what they—I—need to do. I cannot stay with my feelings so much. My awareness clicks off when necessary. I must do that to cope with this new reality, death facing me. Me facing death.

Today I said to Sandy, "You better dance with me now because when I'm dead you'll remember what a good dancer I was." And Sandy cried her eyes out as we danced. I felt bad to have made her so sad, but relieved to have Sandy understand how frightened I am.

Barbara
June 15

I'm back in the hospital again. And just woke from a remarkable dream: Mom felt near me, possibly even taking chemotherapy for me. I woke up with anxiety but feeling intense love for her.

The numbers drift by slowly on the pump. I stare and compute and count. A few more hours, then a few more days. Today I imagined that I would die just around the same time my mother will.

Barbara
June 20

My garden is lovely. The Japanese maple so delicate, the hydrangea opening. I sit here, my dog at my side, staring out at the life in that plot of land, trying to allow myself to be as tired as I am.

Barbara's letter to friends
June 1987

Dear Friends,

When I returned from Florence, I became very depressed because this was the first time that I actually had a symptom that so clearly represented a limitation for me. The new chemotherapy I get is stronger than anything I've had in the past and the effects, too, are worse. The fatigue is overwhelming and now I have other physical side effects, like annoying sensations in my fingers. In order to cope with many of these horrible circumstances and demands on my body and my spirit, I have withdrawn a little bit from life. I am a little more emotionally distant, a little numb, a little depressed.

Depression is foreign to me. I often would get sad, but rarely depressed. Now I occasionally feel deeply depressed and that takes the form of not caring, of being numb, of pulling away. I have always been a very engaged and present person, hardly ever drifting away from people, attachments, commitments, or conversations. Now I have to make space in my life for the feelings of depression that come and go. I have to work at being kind to myself and not being too harsh or judgmental when I have these feelings of shutting off. After all, my unconscious is probably doing me a favor by shutting down and protecting me from all the anger I feel, the overwhelming loss and sadness, and the thousand forms of resentment I must deal with when I compare my situation with that of my contemporaries.

Now I am actively coping with losses, holes, empty spaces, too much time, not enough energy, a future that is uncertain, and a present that rapidly changes. I live from CAT scan to CAT scan, from chemotherapy to chemotherapy. My present is always changing, never stable, and I am required to adjust to news, some-times good, sometimes bad, every month.

This week my doctor gave me a break by postponing chemo-therapy for twelve days. Now I have some energy this week, sand-wiched between treatments. This is now one of the ways I can improve the quality of my life, to have good weeks and a break from chemotherapy, without running the risk of wild cancer growth. I cannot say, Thank God for these little things, anymore. I am angry, furious, resentful. I hate it. I hate how my life has turned into a series of doctor appointments, treatments, side effects, blood tests, CAT scans, liver scans, and bone scans. I have been more hopeful, more optimistic, braver in the past. This stage is more difficult. This feels like an angry time.

I am committed to sharing this process with you, to make it more intelligible, more clear, and more real. To lessen my feelings of isolation. To connect with friends. To tell the truth, no matter how painful that truth may be. The truth is that this is a hard time and I rage against my fate. And another truth is that feelings come and go, fall and rise, manifest themselves and fade, change, become transformed. I am sure that more kinds of feelings will emerge as I pass from stage to stage along this path. I am certainly hoping that lightness and peace will come back soon.

Have the summer you want.

Love,

Barbara

Sandy
July 13

Now a seeming remission. "Life as usual," Barbara says. "I don't want to be a cancer patient twenty-four hours a day." We hire a tutor and begin a French conversation class. Barbara has purchased a classical guitar and begun lessons. I go to my office early each morning, leaving her hunched over the guitar, forehead furrowed, practicing flamenco triplets, wrapped in her red terry cloth bathrobe, bald head glistening. We have little adventures again, together and apart. We relish fresh-ground coffee beans in the morning, the tiny oasis that is our yard in the late afternoon — and most of all, each other.

Barbara
July 18

I'm not angry all the time now. In fact allowing the rage to flow out has enabled me to feel relief. I'm happier and more energetic these last few weeks than in many months.

I'm interested in things again after a long period of having to cope with emergency treatment, the emotional impact of it all, then trying to get back to normal. I could probably cope better if my condition didn't change all the time. I would surely welcome a long period of stability and predictability, but that hasn't been my experience in the last few months. It's been rough water, always changing. Now, at last, the cancer is controlled, my liver is functioning better, and I can rest for a little while.

I'm interested in things again . . . thinking about doing a sociological study on how novelists are selected for publication . . . making arrangements to begin to study the cello and have resumed playing classical guitar again. I had a few music appreciation lessons, which was wonderful. I'm thinking about talking in Yiddish, Spanish, or French a few hours a week, beginning a conversational tutorial. Yiddish seems the most compelling. I'm writing an essay on the importance of judgment, discrimination, and discernment. It is going well and I'm pleased.

I know my liver is functioning normally again because I just lost four pounds, the first weight I have been able to lose since the cancer travelled to my liver. This means the liver is metabolizing correctly. Pounds and water retention mean a bad liver. I'll never be skinny and Camille-ish, even towards the end. My luck to get the kind of cancer that will keep me *zoftig* till the day I die.

I have become tremendously creative at making up twenty-minute projects. Cleaning my library for twenty minutes. Phone calls that last twenty minutes or just enough music for twenty minutes. Sometimes my energy runs out before then. Or my concentration. But right now twenty minutes seems like a perfect amount of time.

Sandy
July 20

Barbara's symptoms now are from the chemotherapy, not the spreading disease, and, consequently, less terrifying. Now we return to our bedrock issue calibrating and recalibrating closeness. She vacillates: be available to me when I'm scared or in pain; leave me alone to feel autonomous and self-sustaining.

I feel most impotent when she is in pain or when she's frightened. I mother her too much, mothering being my most familiar, powerful role. I arrange her among the blankets, rent videos, buy flowers, cook her favorite foods, play her favorite music. My caretaking is too effusive and it is suffocating for both of us. I find it hard just to be with her as she struggles with fear. I want to fix it, to ease it, to soften her tense face. Seeing her vulnerability forces me to face my own. But mostly I turn away from it to tend to her and grow burdensome. She goes so far away when she is in pain: her face tightens and closes; her body stiffens; she cannot speak. I am alone, outside, and am, for the moment, temporarily bereft. Her fear parallels my own, and we cannot do more than hold each other and cry. I whisper to her, "I feel so powerless to help you. I want to take your pain into my body, to give you respite from it." She reaches towards me, touches my face, but her eyes seem inward now, the reflex an automatic one.

Sandy

August 24

We have just returned from a trip into Barbara's past. First to Chicago for several steamy, summer days to attend the annual sociology meetings. We saw many of her old professors and colleagues, and while everyone was delighted to see her, Barbara seemed minimally engaged, watchful. We spent a day at Northwestern, where Deborah, a friend of her student days, now a photographer, joined us. She took pictures of Barbara, who grew more animated then, eagerly pointing to the windows of student apartments, the bakery where she used to get morning pastries, paths by the lake where she had walked and argued with other students. We sat together on a large boulder by the lake, remembering that young girl and her dreams of becoming a sociologist, a teacher. A professional woman.

Then on to Vermont College for faculty meetings. Barbara expanded in this environment, became articulate and emotional with her colleagues. Their passions and commitment to their students and the graduate program reminded her that she had gone to school to become a teacher. Not a professor.

Tomorrow the cycle begins again. Three days in the hospital for chemo, four days at home on the pump. Then we are going to Sea Ranch. I'm greatly in need of quiet walks, the sound of the ocean, the stillness. I need a break from this psychologically exhausting travel for a few days. Just the sea, novels, popcorn, and Barbara.

We fly to London after our return to spend a few weeks and will return for chemo again at the end of the month. It's the same abrupt but determined way she decided to go to Florence. This is the time to say good-bye to the important people in her life. Of course we'll go.

Barbara

September 3

Sandy and I are in Sea Ranch, a coastal development in Northern California that overlooks the ocean, a place where we have spent many holidays over the years. It's always been a contemplative place for me, yet somehow is not as I remember. It was different before I had cancer. My life was so full of people—and so full of travel—that I was exhausted much of the time and coming here was a treat filled with stillness and peace. A place to rest, be quiet, read luxuriously in front of the fire.

Now there is an urgency to write, to visit old friends. I was worried that I might be too agitated to reach stillness, afraid of it. But in this moment, in this place, I am relieved to find I have a great deal of it still inside me.

Sandy and I walk together on familiar trails, past decaying foliage, matted grasses on the side of the road. We cross to the beach, where we come upon a decomposing seal, its odor filling the air. We approach, circle the shell of a once-living thing, and I wonder if I, too, will look that way—so empty—once I am no longer inside myself.

Later in the day, a bird, lost in our house, flies into a window, its illusion of escape, and falls stunned to the floor. Tenderly I place it outside on the grass, hoping it will die rapidly and without pain. But Sandy insists upon taking it to the veterinarian and gently holds it— prolonging its agony and giving it false hope that it can one day fly again.

I drive into town, weeping, as the sparrow is encased in Sandy's loving hands. Every moment of the bird's concussion is pain that I experience in my own body. I cannot find distance from the bird. I, too, am stunned.

It is heartbreakingly sweet, with the cutest face. It has been a long time since I held a bird. A very long time since I held a dying bird. And an even longer time since I've read my Darwin. But there are examples in the natural world. The seal and sparrow are two. I'm only a third. I collapse in sobs when the whole episode is over, recovering the torn edges of myself from the paralyzed, soon-to-die, young, baby bird.

Living in an
Unstable Body

Barbara

My doctor put it to me very clearly: I had to have chemotherapy, surgery, and radiation, in that order. I had to have chemotherapy for three months before surgery because the tumor in my breast was too large to remove surgically. It had grown too quickly and was now virtually inoperable. Chemotherapy would shrink the tumor, permitting surgery without skin graft. There was another reason for chemotherapy first: the cancer had spread to my lymph nodes, including a supraclavicular node near my collarbone. That was an indicator that metastatic processes were already occurring throughout my body. It was a serious, aggressive cancer and I would require the most aggressive treatment available.

Before the first treatment, my doctor prepared me for the various side effects I might experience: my hair would fall out; I'd have mouth sores; I'd vomit; and I'd lose my period. So after the first treatment, I vomited about thirty times in forty-eight hours, had tired muscles and aching joints, and was exhausted from spasmodic vomiting. And that was just the first week.

The second week, I had low blood counts, extreme fatigue, and breathlessness from the lack of sufficient hemoglobin—and consequently oxygen—in my blood. Almost exactly on the twenty-first day following the first set of three injections, my hair began to fall out. Not just on my head. I lost my pubic hair as well. But I still had my period.

After the second treatment, I had all the side effects again. And I still had my period. I thought for sure I'd beat this: I wouldn't go into menopause.

Following the third treatment, I had all the same side effects but, this time, I had a shorter period. Still I didn't attend to it much because, by this time, my nose and anus were bleeding from chemotherapy and I had grown alarmed. It seemed like I was bleeding from new places and losing the familiar bleeding from familiar places.

Three weeks later, after the fourth treatment, my period stopped. I began to get hot flashes, sometimes as frequently as one an hour. My ears glowed bright red, my face darkened, and sweat collected on the surface of my skin. I felt like a vibrating tuning fork for the next two minutes. Then my internal air conditioning took over, but didn't know when to stop. I got cold; I'd quickly cover myself to avoid the chill of perspiration. I could never find the right amount of clothing because my internal thermostat was completely out of balance. I no longer had any sense of what "room temperature"—that euphemism for a shareable external reality—was. I had no reliable information from my body about the temperature of the outside world. My only information, which I knew was distorted and unreliable, came from deep inside my body.

Then all the hair on my head fell out. Frantically I searched for a good wig before this occurred, but nothing fit my small head. I found a hairdresser who worked for the opera company and he used his connections to get a wig for me. The wig fit but felt foreign and made my scalp hot and itchy. I decided, like many other women who become bald from chemotherapy, not to disguise my loss.

Hats now hang off any available hook in my apartment. I have cotton hats, wool hats, berets, hats with brims, ski caps. Friends have knitted caps for me. And, even now, every time I go into the street, I'm still aware that people look at me. A vital aspect of my social identity has been taken away. In the last six months, I've lost my hair twice. And before that, three times. Practice does not make it easier.

Losing my hair has been much harder than losing my breast. No one can see underneath my clothes. But everyone can see my hair. I never thought my hair was beautiful: it was a simple, brown mop that I combed and washed. It grew out of my scalp. It was a part of me. It was mine.

But as I saw it cover my pillow, as I saw gobs of it come out on the comb, and masses of it clog the shower drain, I sank powerlessly into resignation.

I knew my hair would grow back when I went off the powerful chemotherapy to another combination of chemicals. It did, but thinly. And then I went off chemotherapy completely and all my hair came back, thick and spiky. But during that time when I didn't take chemotherapy, the cancer spread to my liver and then my lungs. I had to have chemotherapy, the strong stuff, again. Now it is clear that I will never have a full head of hair again. I now lose my hair once a month. I will always look like a Buddhist monk until the day I die.

My pudenda is as smooth as a fig. Even a peach with its infantile fuzziness is too hairy to describe it. Bald, completely smooth except for one Fu Manchu-like hair, straight and long, that resisted decimation. It is a dark, sturdy branch that extends from my skin. It is my mysterious hair, this proud survivor.

Losing my pubic hair, I felt naked and embarrassed, inadvertently returned to pre-pubescence. I was too exposed and didn't want to be touched.

My vagina was changing too. The vaginal tissue was thinning and becoming more sensitive to pressure and friction. It began to hurt when Sandy and I had sex. Then I noticed that my ordinary levels of dampness seemed to be changing: I was becoming less moist. Worst of all I stopped lubricating when I became sexually excited. That single, physiological fact made me realize that the agreements and understandings I had with my body were no longer in effect. If I no longer lubricated when I got sexually aroused, then how could I know I was feeling sexy?

Until I began chemotherapy, my relationship with my body was simple, direct, and uncomplicated. I had a friendly, warm, and pleasurable relationship with my body. Sex was always fun and untroubled. The cycles of my ability to become aroused were exquisitely dependent on my hormones. Ten days before my period, like clockwork, I would begin to feel sexual. This would continue for the next ten days and when my period came the urge would fizzle out. In other words, I had a physiologically based definition of my own sexual excitement: if my body produced some of the sensations that, through experience, had become my standard set of signals for sexual excitement, then I knew what to do with my behavior. But when chemotherapy induced an early and rapidly onsetting menopause and my hormone levels dropped dramatically, I was no longer on a monthly hormone cycle. I could no longer tell when I felt sexy or premenstrual. I got very confused about what I was feeling and when I was feeling it.

These questions of semantic meaning were urgently pre-empted by the necessity of finding practical solutions. Without body clues to signal me as to when and how I was feeling sexy, I consulted my head. Sandy and I recreated situations that had a proven record of creating the right mood in me. We purposefully incorporated the old, reliable environmental cues that had worked so well in the past: excellent food, candlelight, intimate conversation, music. I felt as close as could be, but nothing was happening in my body. We tried romantic meals at cozy restaurants. Nothing. Massage with scented oils. Nothing. Morning hiking in the country followed by steaming coffee and good pancakes. Nothing. Everything in my head told me this should be the right moment to make love but there were no signals coming from my body. Sandy touched me in all the loving, familiar ways. It was soothing and pleasant but not sexy. Nothing. The conclusion: for me sex does not work in the head.

We stopped making love. Instead we found new ways of being intimate. Sandy, who is a very light sleeper and consequently sleeps far away from me so as not to be disturbed by my twists and turns, began to hold me through the night. Our hands found new ways to console each other. I was reminded of how animals touch, lick, and chew each other. They pick at and groom each other, making the other feel secure and loved with their paws. I would touch Sandy's throat in a spot I knew contained all her tears: she would sob. And right in the midst of chemotherapy infusions, when the chemicals were flowing into my veins from huge syringes, Sandy helped me relax by touching my back and neck lightly.

I confess I was still nervous about not making love. Without telling Sandy I still tried to make myself feel sexy. I believed that if I tried hard enough, I could discover a more subtle sexual language in my body. I thought maybe I could pick up these signals when alone. So when Sandy was busy or out of the house, I tried to get in the mood to masturbate. Nothing. But our new intimacy helped ease the passage. I accepted this nonsexual period as part of my life. Ultimately the rock bottom question remains: when facing one's own death, what happens to one's sexuality? I suppose for some women sexual feelings become intensified. They become hungry for life, hungry for life through sex. Erotic energy keeps them alive. I suspect Sandy would have liked it better if I experienced the life force as erotic energy, as libido. But I don't. My life energy comes in another form, in the passion to learn everything, to feel everything, to live every moment with presence and intensity. To study new things. To master new areas of knowledge. To write—alone and with Sandy. Together we have developed a new form that can accommodate our individual and unique voices into a dialogue. We write about things that are important to us. We make love at the typewriter, not in the bedroom.

As I write now, I see that I was learning a new language of the body but it was the language of symptoms, not of sexuality. I became sensitive to when my body was retaining water. I could glance at my various parts, my legs, arms, stomach, and chest and notice a puffiness that had not been there the day before. I learned that when I became puffy, my metabolism was off and that meant my liver wasn't functioning properly. I calculated the ebbs and flows of my energy because my daily activities, as simple as taking a walk, depended on an exact calibration of that energy. I observed how it wavered, how much time I had between the waves, how it disappeared all at once, without forewarning. I discovered how close I could come to throwing up without actually having to do it. I studied the gradations of nausea and their subdivisions, and how to assess when nausea would pass or when I had to take an anti-nausea pill. I learned how to move quickly to the curb while walking the dog, emptying the contents of my stomach there, not on the sidewalk, and how to look reasonably dignified afterward. I learned how to run fast while compressing my anal sphincter muscles so that I wouldn't shit in my pants from the diarrhea that chemo induced. Sometimes I didn't make it.

In the last two and a half years, I peed in my pants three times. Chemotherapy irritates the bladder. That's why doctors tell you to drink half a gallon of liquid whenever you get chemotherapy. The chemicals are so strong that they can even cause cancer of the bladder. On the few occasions I couldn't control my urine, I noticed that I didn't get the usual signal that told me it was time to think about going to the bathroom. It didn't begin as a small pressure or urge, as it normally does, and then build up. No, rather it came on with a burst of urgency, as if I'd been holding it for hours. I had to learn this new language too.

The form of my body changed too. I lost a breast. When I had the mastectomy, I was too worried about my life to worry about my breast. I hoped that the doctors would "get" all the cancer in my breast and that postoperative radiation would control any errant cells that had not been excised by surgery. Losing a breast did alter my body image, as well as my body, but I never felt a diminishment of my femininity. My breasts were never the center of my womanness.

From the responses of other women in my support group and also from my cancer counselor, I knew that losing a breast was very hard for some women. In my cancer support group, most women were concerned about reconstructive surgery. They swapped names of good plastic surgeons. They talked about aesthetic criteria for evaluating a good job, such as the surgeon's ability to make breasts match in color, tone, weight, density, shape, and identicality of nipple placement with appropriate tones of darkness. To me, they expressed a fetishistic quality in their talk; they were desperate and afraid.

One woman in the support group told the story of someone whose husband left her from the time of the mastectomy until she got her reconstructed breast. She explained matter-of-factly that he couldn't bear the sight of his wife. Then there's the letter I got from a distant acquaintance who told me that she, too, had had breast cancer. She wrote that it wasn't so dangerous now that they could control it with early detection. She also wrote that, since her surgery a few years before, she, herself, never got undressed in front of her husband. When they made love, she always wore her bra with the prosthesis tucked inside.

I couldn't even imagine how these women might feel about their partners. I would feel enraged. I cannot count the number of stories I've heard about couples, both lesbian and straight, breaking up after a mastectomy. Illness places enormous strains on couples and many separate afterwards. Each person may feel guilt and abandonment simultaneously.

I'm very lucky. Sandy has been exceptionally steadfast and easy about the changes in my body. She did not compel me to pay attention to her needs, her anxieties, her worries. She never made me feel inadequate or freakish. Her face never revealed shock or terror. She was easy with my scar, touching it delicately. During vomiting bouts she simply got the bucket, never cringing or complaining. She was always softly, gently there, through everything.

Signals about hunger also got confused when I began chemotherapy. Up until that time, food was one of the great pleasures of my life. Over the years I'd become very sophisticated about food and very knowledgeable about its preparation. Eating was a supremely aesthetic experience for me. I always tried to eat and cook well for myself. Unlike many people who don't cook for themselves when they are alone, I didn't need the company of another person to stimulate me to cook: my own pleasure was sufficient. I would cook sweetbreads in a cream sauce or chicken with lemon and tarragon. Tastes would explode on my tongue, clear and definite tastes.

So when chemotherapy caused painful sores in my mouth and the only thing I could consume was a blenderful of fruit and yogurt, I became despondent. It hurt even to put solid food in my mouth. My appetite and desire for particular flavors and sensations was annihilated. I could no longer tell when I was hungry or when I wanted a specific texture or flavor. All I wanted to do was to get the food down and keep it down and to make sure it didn't hurt as I ate. I treated myself like a hospital patient, making an eating schedule and sticking to it, making sure I had enough protein, liquid, and caloric content.

Now there is never a time in my treatment cycle when my mouth isn't sore or sensitive. I can't have spices—I can't eat hot Chinese food or savor my favorite cuisine, Indian food. My diet resembles that of an ulcer patient: bland and creamy. My relationship to food has been permanently altered and I grieve this loss every day.

In the last two years, my clothes have increased by three sizes. My legs filled with fluid and were puffy and large. My arms and shoulders, usually slender, looked bulky and strong. I remember when Sandy and I saw a beautiful pair of green loafers in a shop window in Amsterdam. They were the first expensive, European shoes I ever owned, but I can no longer wear them. My feet became swollen with fat and fluids. I consulted Shizuko Yamamoto, a well-known macrobiotic practitioner in New York. She slapped my thighs and said in a thick accent, "Water jugs, your legs are like water jugs."

I watched my body stretch to accommodate all the fluid that was collecting in my tissues. I could not believe how rapidly my body shape was changing. I needed new clothes immediately, but going shopping was a horrendous experience. Sandy was kind and patient. She had reached her full height of six feet by the age of thirteen and shopping for clothes that didn't fit was a familiar experience. Turning what was humiliating into an adventure was an old defense for her and now served us both well. I'd be crying from frustration in the fitting room and Sandy would quietly leave and cheerfully return with a few items in the next size.

One day I stopped going to department stores. It was too hard. I decided to go to a shop for larger women. While walking to it, I passed a maternity shop and thought that these clothes might fit me. They did.

The surface of my skin changed too. My veins became more prominent because the fluid in my tissues pressed them against my skin. Even the tiniest capillaries started bursting and my skin became marbled with designs. On my inner thighs, where the pressure was greatest, the capillaries looked like calligraphy. My body oils disappeared and my skin became parched and crusty. Flakes of skin fell from my face. My fingernails first turned black from chemotherapy, then they became ridged with white bands. My fingernails became like alum, soft and whitish, and they ripped rather than broke.

Two and a half years since the first diagnosis and I am still getting chemotherapy six days a month. For two days I'm in the hospital, where I get Adriamycin, and for four days I'm attached to an ambulatory pump filled with Velban, another type of chemotherapy. It hangs from my waist on a velcro belt, buttressed by a safety pin. It looks like a Walkman. Tubes extend from its square form into a one-inch needle that is inserted into my chest. It is attached to a Port-A-Cath, a plastic container that is surgically placed in my chest, the purpose of which is to receive chemotherapy. My veins are too fragile and unstable. They've stabbed me too many times and missed. They have had too many veins burst open with gushing blood. The chemo has burned my veins too many times, making them fibrotic and painfully sensitive.

When I wear the portable pump, I am bombarded by images: of being attached to a bomb, having an artificial limb, having additional plumbing, like there's a giant opening in me, like it's a bionic extension. It's like having shrapnel inside you, like an artificial hip or a metal plate instead of your skull.

My hand rests on the pump: I sense its vibrations and hear it churning along. With the aid of Valium and sleeping pills, I sleep with it tied to my waist. It runs on batteries. It is saving my life. Other people wear pumps too: diabetics get insulin, older people get liquid nutrition, people with AIDS get antibiotics, and people with intractable pain get a continuous infusion of painkilling drugs like morphine. I have cancer and I get chemotherapy. I hate the pump.

Yesterday I called a woman who is on the pump all the time, 24 hours a day, 365 days a year, getting chemotherapy for liver cancer. She was helpful and gave me words of encouragement. Maybe I can learn from her.

What is it like to live in a body that keeps on changing? It's frightening, terrifying, and confusing. It generates a feeling of helplessness. It produces a slavish attention to the body. It creates an unnatural hypervigilance toward any and all sensations that occur within the landscape of the body. One becomes a prisoner to any perceptible change in the body, any cough, any difference in sensation. One loses one's sense of stability and predictability, as well as one's sense of control over the body. It forces you to give up the idea that you can will the body to behave in ways you would like. Predictability ends. One grieves over its loss, and that further complicates the process of adjustment to an unstable body. Time becomes shortened and is marked by the space between symptoms.

In our culture it is very common to rely on the body as the ultimate arbiter of truth. We consult our bodies like an oracle. While every emotion may not be consciously available to be experienced, the body knows the truth. We cannot conceal the truth from the body.

We turn to the body to decipher its coded language, to apprehend its grammar and syntax. By noticing the body's responses to situations, we have an idea about how we "really feel about things." For example, if you get knots in your stomach every time a certain person walks into the room, you have an important body clue to investigate. Or if your eyes tear up during a yawn, you might suspect that you may be experiencing some deep and underlying sadness that has not yet come to the surface or, as Wordsworth put it, a thought too deep for tears.

We trust that the body will tell us the truth about emotions that are hidden from consciousness. We trust that the body knows things before the mind does. Our job is to mind the body, to mine the body, to interpret its language.

Interpretations of bodily signals are premised on the uninterrupted stability and continuity of the body. We experience the continuity of the body as taken for granted. Only when there are interruptions does the body become problematic. We usually associate the same continuous sensations with the same stimulations. When the body, like my body, is no longer consistent over time, when it gives different signals every month, when something that meant one thing in April may have a different meaning in May, then it's hard to rely on the stability—and therefore the truth—of the body. And because of that, it's hard to interpret and hard to predict.

I was thrown into a crisis of meaning. I could no longer assess and evaluate what sensations meant. I could no longer measure the intensity of sensations. I was no longer fluent in the language of my body, its signs and symbols, and I felt lost.

Living in the world has become an existential problem for me. How to interpret my very existence is problematic. Am I living because I am alive? Am I dying because I'd be dead in three months without chemotherapy? Am I living and dying? Are all of us living and dying, except that I'm doing it faster?

And all of this confusion is predicated on time because the human mind can experience the simultaneity of the past and the present and can project into the future. The human mind has memory. Time past can color the present and the future. If there were only present time, I could joyfully embrace my body and delight in whatever it brings, whatever form it takes, whatever is given to me. If there were only the past, I would remember swimming naked six months after my surgery in the Pacific waters off the coast of Australia's Great Barrier Reef, when my body, without breast, without much hair, looked whole, healthy, and perfect.

If there were only time past. I remember the time Sandy and I went away with friends of ours who were fighting all weekend. We were at a loss. What could we do to make them stop? Distancing myself from their anger, I put on some old Motown music and started dancing. I had just come out of the hot tub and there I was, naked as a jaybird, having a wonderful time, laughing, singing, and dancing unselfconsciously to rock and roll. There I was, with one breast flopping, and one big body dancing. Our friends, stunned at what they called "the life force," stopped fighting and started dancing.

But there is not just the past and not just the present. There is the future. And I can imagine worse scenarios with just as much vividness as I can remember the past. I can envision more chemotherapy, more tubes, more degeneration of body function, more loss of energy and loss of control, more desperation. There may be more physical pain, more ambiguous sensations arising from a body I can no longer interpret, more confusion.

When you have cancer, the body no longer contains the old truths about the world. Instead you must learn a new language, a new vocabulary, and over time, as symptoms converge and conflate, you learn the deeper structure of its grammar. The patient's task is to learn the new language, hoping that the body will remain stable enough. You can no longer rely on the previous systems of interpreting the body you have used before. When you have cancer, the ground is pulled out from under you. Existence is problematic and anxious. You must look for new, stable ground.

When you have cancer, you have a new body each day, a body that may or may not have a relationship to the body you had the day before. When you have cancer, you are bombarded by sensations from within that are not anchored in meaning. They float in a world without words, without meanings. You don't know from moment to moment whether to call a particular sensation a "symptom" or a "side effect" or a "sign." It produces extreme anxiety to be unable to distinguish those sensations that are caused by the disease and those that are caused by the treatment. Words and their referents are uncoupled, uncongealed, no longer connected. You live in a mental world where all the information you have is locked into the present moment. The past, what the doctors may call "your medical history," is useless and irrelevant for your construction of meanings. Sensations come and go; they disappear for a while and they return; they change. They may add up to something; they may not. They may have meaning; they may not. That pain in my stomach may mean something new or it may not. I must wait until something else happens, until I have an accretion of evidence, until a pattern emerges, if I'm lucky enough to have a pattern. Interpretation of a sensation always depends on having at least two bodily events close enough in time to make meaning of seemingly random events. And most of the time, I live in a world of random body events. I'm hostage to the capriciousness of my body, a body that sabotages my sense of a continuous and taken-for-granted reality.

Sometimes I can hardly use human language to tell how I feel. When I am frightened or feel alone and can't sleep, I need to take sleeping pills because I lie there thinking about dying. I explain to Sandy, "If I were a dog, I'd be shaking and trembling." Animals don't use words; their bodies speak for them. While I'm not mute, I am often frustrated by the way the limits of language circumscribe my ability to communicate events in my body. But I am not an animal. I am a human being, an articulate one at that, who is challenged to find words to apply to sensations I've never had before, challenged to find meaning and stability despite a changing body. I'm caught in a relentless metamorphosis. You cannot imagine how stable and firm and fixed your body looks to me. You cannot imagine that I can actually feel my molecules moving around, wondering what miraculous shape they will prefer next time.

LIVING IN MY CHANGING
BODY — AND HERS

Sandy

I begin writing this sitting at the kitchen table drinking tea and listening to the eager clacking of Barbara's typing. She has just begun to write a piece about her changing relationship to her body and has announced quite firmly that she wants to write it alone. I chafe, wishing we could work together, wondering what she will write about our sex life, our changing intimacies. Wanting to be included.

Last week I spoke at the Women's Building about sexuality in the relationship of a couple dealing with life-threatening illness. My talk was very well received and many of the women seemed relieved to hear me describe the physical or emotional isolation they were experiencing. I was both moved by and grateful for the response and it deepened my conviction that the writing Barbara and I are doing is vital in the lives of others who are living through many of the same realities.

I spoke about our sex life: how it used to be, how it is now, how we have accommodated to the physical changes in Barbara's body, the emotional changes in her psyche, and the relational changes in our daily lives. I didn't talk like that though.

I talked in a daily language. One of need and dependency. Mostly mine. Of an inwardness and sometimes excruciating thoughtfulness. Mostly hers. I talked about the way I was socialized to be an appropriate heterosexual and had lived for nearly thirty-five years in response to the sexual needs of others, and how hard I had struggled against that early conditioning when I came out as a lesbian. I spoke of how easily I find myself slipping back into those old roles again. How I find myself feeling Barbara's needs are the real needs and that mine are not. That her feelings are the ones that matter, and mine don't. That the frequency, the form, the intensity of the sexual dimension of our lives will—no—should be determined by her. Not by me and rarely by us. Just like it was before when I was in my twenties and thirties. Actually I know it isn't like before, but I do admit to an uneasy similarity sometimes.

Now I sit wishing she would call to me from her office down the hall and ask me what I would add to her piece. What is it like for me, as her partner? How does it feel to live with a woman who now has advanced cancer spreading through her body?

If she did ask, I would begin by writing about her breast. The one they excised soon after her diagnosis. The surgeon and the oncologist, both women, remarked after the surgery was over that we seemed to be "handling" the experience so well. I think what they meant was that we were not acting like some heterosexual couples. Barbara expressed no shame about "disfigurement," no embarrassment about being less of a woman, or worry that desire would never return. Unlike many husbands I did not awkwardly avert my glance from her wound but, instead, kissed her scar, her chest and her body after the surgery with the same love, passion, tenderness that I had before. She was still Barbara. This was still the body of the woman I had loved all those years. It was only that the body had assumed a different shape. Quieter now. More mood swings. But she was still Barbara inside herself.

Then I would write about the loss of her pubic hair and how unusual it was for me to see her vulva exposed in that way. I had been shaved twice in preparation for the birth of my two daughters nearly thirty years ago but had never seen another adult woman without hair. I found myself intrigued at the odd juxtaposition of a girlish pudenda and a woman's body. I wanted to touch and stroke it but she was uncomfortable and wouldn't allow me to. The hair on her head was gone, too, which caused her more public shyness and uncertainty. But the loss of pubic hair made her feel like a child, utterly vulnerable and exposed. It was not possible for her to open further — to open beyond the vulnerability of her body being so uncovered, so unprotected.

Then I would write about her edema. How her body became swollen with fluids that were not being processed properly by her liver. Barbara gained twenty-five pounds in barely a month. She described her body as being unfamiliar and alien: bloated, hairless, and always with some level of discomfort, weakness, achiness, or nausea — the endless variety of symptoms chemotherapy produces in the body.

At first I was unthinkingly delighted as her hips spread and grew wider. I reassured her that her hips (indeed hips in general), were my favorite part of a woman's body. Bigger hips meant, to me at least, better hips. I found her body very exciting and was filled with renewed desire. She, however, felt trapped and alienated in this stranger's body and was unable or unwilling to respond.

She has just come down the hall carrying the pages she has written. As I read them my eyes fill with tears of recognition. I read how she experiences us making love at the typewriter. How each morning we would walk laboriously to my office, resting every few blocks, and sit beside each other, one of us at the keyboard, the other sitting closely alongside. We typed, interrupted, criticized, added, paced, drank coffee, laughed, then grew thoughtful, intense, or joyous with relief when just the right word or image emerged. It was a making of love. An honoring of our bond. Lovemaking. The work we did had the focus, the passion, the sense of completion our lovemaking once had. I often felt similarly spent when a work session ended. But so loved. So known. So deeply connected to this woman.

In rereading these thoughts about my response to Barbara's changing body, I notice that I am present only in response, in relationship to Barbara. As her body changes, as her needs, strength, and focus shift—I respond. I notice now, for the first time, that, slowly, imperceptibly, gradually, Barbara's body has become the body in our lives. I have ceased to have a body and, instead, have Barbara's. Her stamina, her vitality, her appetites delineate our day. When we awoke, if she felt strong enough for a long walk, we would walk. If she felt sluggish or weak, the morning would be spent in a more sedentary way—reading, writing, visiting with friends. When her appetite was good and there were none of the monthly mouth sores making anything but creamy shakes impossible, we would go to eat spicy, ethnic food. When she was unable to, or had lost the appetite for complex flavors, we ate very little and simply, at home.

I, too, have put on a lot of weight but never noticed. I never felt full, or overly full, or stuffed, or bloated, or sated. I cannot remember thinking about if I was hungry, what I wanted to eat, or when I had had enough. We ate. We filled our body with what we liked when we were hungry.

I exercised in relation to Barbara's body. I ate in relation to Barbara's appetite. I had somehow neglected to make a parallel assessment of my own energy, my own desires, my own need for fresh air and exercise. Just as I had been "responsive to her sexual needs," I had become an extension of her physical capacities. Mornings when I had awakened and done yogic stretches had stopped, and I didn't remember why. The feeling of being strong and vital in my body has evaporated as well. I can't remember the last time I felt powerful, the last time my skin tingled with the rush of blood that comes from vigorous exercise.

In much the same way her sexuality has become "our" sexuality—now her body has become "our" body. If she couldn't have a strong, powerful, healthy body—then I simply wouldn't have one either. At least insofar as I could encourage that sameness. It felt impossible to leave Barbara, feeling weak or depleted, reading quietly on the sofa, while I went out to exercise or swim. It felt impossible to enjoy and delight in my body—an act of disloyalty. I can no longer take my body for granted and assume that it will be reliable, strong, and healthy since Barbara can no longer do that, feel that, have that possibility. Even the thought fills me with guilt.

The guilt of survival. The guilt of comparison. The guilt of randomness—being selected out as the one of us who will outlast the other. The one of us who will live beyond the "us" that has been the foundation of my life. The guilt of the relief that it is not me. But what is the same for both of us is that the illusion of endless time no longer exists. There is not going to be enough time for her. And there may not be for me. I no longer imagine my life as an old woman but hope I live long enough to become an old woman. No certainty remains.

I remember how shaken and guilty I felt when she was misdiagnosed. The guilt of having been impatient with what I felt was her hypochondriacal pattern of going to the doctor over "every little thing," a pattern all the women in my family have followed. It was only when her breast started to swell and the lump was clearly palpable that I began to take it as seriously as I should have. Going with her to the Kaiser clinic, I saw the passivity of the patients, the waiting, the fear of taking too much time, of asking too many questions, of being a "nuisance." I felt guilty that I hadn't encouraged her to have her own doctor. A private doctor. That I had ignored her complaints until they were too advanced to contain.

I suppose it is always necessary to rewrite history—to replay a series of "what if," "if only," "how could I have not seen" questions that are the inevitable outgrowth of illness and accidents. I'm no different in this effort to impose retrospective meaning and responsibility. The doctors were responsible. Not me. But I hadn't paid enough attention. I hadn't listened clearly enough to her words. Somehow it was my fault that this was happening to her body. And because it was my fault, I began to deny my own body and my pleasure in it as well.

I have guilty feelings about my thick, heavy, rapidly growing hair. During our ceremony of commitment, now nearly seven months ago, Barbara expressed dismay over her patchy, balding, very short, thin hair.

"It's not as unattractive as you imagine," I assured her.

"Oh?" she responded tartly. "If it's so attractive, why haven't you cut your hair to look like mine?" Hours later I remembered her words, and even though I knew they were said in irritation and frustration, I decided to have my hair cut as a gesture of love and support. When I look back over the photograph album of our ceremony, we both have near crewcuts, decorated with festive earrings and glowing faces.

But now she is bald again and has been for many months, and my hair is growing out—a luxuriant and lovely shade of salt and pepper. I am aware of closing the bathroom door when I brush it and being very careful to take all the hair out of the drain in the shower when I shampoo.

But there is also the gratitude that balances my loss. Gratitude that I can call home and hear her voice rise with eagerness at the sound of my voice. That her sculpted, hairless skull contains her piercing eyes without brows, without lashes. Her unadorned face smiles at the phone when she hears my voice. She is still there inside her changing body—the body so different from the body I first touched and held. One breast, still high and firm. I have two breasts, somewhat fallen and considerably less firm. My body, too, has changed, grown older, and softened. We have become clearer to each other and to ourselves though, our bodies less opaque. We can see through, into each other. We are living in changed and changing bodies—living with full hearts and open minds and great love.

Taking Leave

September 1987 – January 1988

Barbara
September 15

I try to accept the idea that this indeed may be my last trip to Europe. My last really "important" long trip. The plane has just taken off and we face nine and a half hours of flying time to London. How will I do? Will I only be able to take shorter trips in the future? To New York, Santa Fe, or Los Angeles? I don't think it's possible for the human mind to really understand and accept the finality of the "last trip." The "last" time to see anyone. There is always a dream, always a wish, always a hope that there will be another time and another place. Things can't just end. They can't stop. I can't simply disappear.

Sandy
September 15

We crisscross climates, urban and rural landscapes, and alternate trips filled with people with those of solitude and reflection. Our time is filled now with the fullness of what we create together—the synergy that crackles and draws others towards us. And each day carries with it the inevitable moment when everyone abruptly remembers the fact that Barbara is dying. Sometimes it is the painful awkwardness of using the wrong verb tense. At others, it is the unpredictable exhaustion that washes over her, leaving her spent as she awkwardly excuses herself to lie down. These moments mock us, hovering just outside every interaction now. But Barbara and I continue to name her death, insist upon incorporating it into our lives, live with it. How many of us have such intimate relationships with our specters?

Sandy
September 22

This is a very exhausting time for Barbara. She careens from nostalgia to enthusiasm, from reminiscence to melancholy each day. Old friends come to visit and each releases a torrent of history, of feeling.

We are staying in Michelle and Ruth's generous home filled with books, children, intellectual passions, a clutter of lifetimes. Its richness and their love of Barbara fill me.

Riek and Ingrid, who were with us less than a year ago at our ceremony of commitment, travelled from Amsterdam to visit us in London. We reconnected with an ease that belied the months since we were last all together.

But beneath the surface, the loving feels so desperate. I have just removed my flawlessly constructed false nails, the nails that were to cover the chewed fingers beneath them. The chewed fingers that were a visible symbol of my fear and impotence. The nails I chew without noticing, as I once smoked cigarettes. I needed to appear intact on this journey. No frayed edges, no raw skin. No chipped, broken, damaged me.

Sandy
September 24

We have just spent several hours looking at illuminated Persian manuscripts at Maggs Brothers on Berkeley Square. Barbara's sense of reverence at being in such a place and her boisterous enthusiasm battled for primacy. The latter won. I sat on a bench and watched her as she opened drawers filled with images, drawings, engravings, manuscript pages, and old documents, asking questions of the staff, losing herself in this new world. Then, after a while, she looked over at the whispering collectors. "Hi," she smiled at them. "Hi, whaddya looking at?" They, warming to her guilelessness, and she to their response, chattered for nearly an hour in this small room as I sat alone by the window, looking out at the sun-warmed benches below. Barbara bought an example of Ottoman calligraphy and two pages of Persian manuscript. I will hang them by her bed when we return home so she can enjoy them there, close to her.

Barbara
September 26

This trip kept illness away. Women I love, books, Scandinavian cuisine, and drinking twice in one week, after not drinking for almost six months. But this trip did not keep feelings away, nor memories, nor loss.

The last good-byes said at the airport, final embraces over, Sandy and I turned the corner leading to passport control and I began to cry. Sandy quietly placed her hand on my back for comfort. We had transformed a friendship between Michelle and me into a quartet, becoming friends as couples. They were so good to us, so caring, so attentive to detail, and sensitive to mood.

We talked of futures, concrete futures, and it gives me hope and a dream. A book review in three weeks; another article to keep me alive for five weeks; another trip in December: a dream good for three months.

No, there is no last trip. See you again. See you in December. Oh God, please stay alive. Oh God, let me live until December, able to travel. Marking futures together, times together. My toast last night, "Till the next time."

Barbara
November 10

I have loved many people and have been well loved in my life. During this difficult period of decline, their love sustains me. I cannot imagine facing death without being surrounded by love. I have spent the last six months re-tracing my steps, re-igniting old contacts with those whom I once loved. I can and have loved many people simultaneously, each for different reasons, different qualities—for who I became when I was with that person, for the qualities they brought out in me.

My personal history has involved a chain of people I have loved. Until I met Sandy, when, in the name of monogamy, I stopped taking lovers. But during these past years, I have been able to love other people quite intensely while continuing to be faithful to Sandy. I savor all these loves because I have come to understand that loving one person does not mean another is less loved or less compelling. I've learned to love positively, not having to tarnish and spoil one love in order to have another. The advantages of age, I suppose.

I am sad when I think about my life being over. Sometimes the sadness consumes me more than my cancer. I no longer regret not having had children. But one means that I have found to create a sense of immortality is the creation of love in another where there was none before. That I have loved and been loved and that my work is of use to others, these are my two greatest accomplishments. It's true. Love and work are what matter.

Barbara
November 18

Steam spurts through the radiator. It's November. My wet fingers are wrapped in a towel. The task is complete. Two perfect amaryllis bulbs sit in plastic containers. My twenty-month-old nephew will watch his first flowers grow, bloom, and die. He will watch and laugh sweetly. The process will take three or four months. Their petals will fall in early spring.

Soon it will be February. And it will be three years that I have lived since the day of my diagnosis. I didn't think I had so much time and now the air chills too often for me to avoid: the end is nearer.

Barbara's letter to friends
December 1987

Dear Friends,

This is the season for miracles: the miracle of light, symbolized by the *Chanukah* candles; the miracle of darkness, symbolized by the winter solstice; and the miracle of a paradigmatically loving life, as symbolized by the birth of Christ.

I have my own miracle as well. It has been one year since the breast cancer spread to my liver. With the help of chemotherapy, the cancer has been controlled. Although it has not shrunk, it has not grown either and that enables me to peacefully co-exist with it. I am celebrating the holiday season and the three-year anniversary since my diagnosis with good cheer and optimism. My logic is this: if the chemo has been working up until now, who knows how long it will continue to work? Maybe that's my miracle. I've seen friends die this year with diagnoses far less serious than mine. By all logic and statistics, I should have been the first to die. But I am still here. I have finally reached the point where everything I've been trained to think about prediction is useless; knowledge cannot tell me why I am living so well and living so long, despite major metastases to the liver and lung. I have entered a crisis of knowledge, a sort of epistemological anxiety and have learned that my own internal life is a much more reliable source of knowledge than external information.

As a consequence the issues I focus on in therapy now have a philosophic and reflective bias. This therapeutic work has been very significant in terms of keeping me emotionally clear and thoughtful about the values and commitments I bring to this period of my life. It has become clear to me that being a human being, as opposed to any sort of label that ends in "ologist," is the hardest thing in the world to do. Allowing one's humanity to be touched in an ongoing way; allowing people to be themselves, without judgment or wishing a change in outcome; allowing oneself to be filled with the self and, paradoxically, to be a vessel; creating expansion and space in one's heart and yet not letting it collapse from the weight of its own tenderness and despair—these are all aspects of my understanding of what it means to be human. I think for the first time that I can be consoled by life. Before I was inconsolable because of my illness. There is nothing that shocks me anymore because I have let go of many preconceptions and expectations. I can now bend in the wind.

How will you spend your year? I hope with love, energy, fascination, delight, calm, strength, intensity, contemplation, reflection, and creativity.

The theme of this letter is miracles. May there be many miracles this year in your life. May you be open enough to see them. May I continue to have the miracle of life.

With love,

Barbara

Sandy
December 18

Again, just as this time last year, Kathy Grant called to tell us that Barbara's liver functioning seemed unusual. If her tumor is growing again, there is no longer any chemotherapy to hold it in check. Barbara has been taking Adriamycin for the past three years, and while it has controlled the spread of cancer, it apparently hasn't shrunk the tumor in her liver at all. Now she can no longer take it because she has already reached maximum dosage and any more would be toxic.

Barbara has been experiencing suggestive changes in her body: a sense of fullness after eating only a small amount of food; a feeling of being swollen around her middle, although her weight is the same. Her internal thermostat is untrustworthy; she swings from very hot to very cold without running a fever and without any change in the external environment. So when the doctor said she had an elevated liver count, Barbara already "knew" that something was wrong. She had an internal, almost cellular, sense that in the final analysis is trustworthy and reliable. She knew her liver had enlarged. The doctor merely confirmed it.

Sandy
December 19

Barbara has only a few months to live now. The cancer has begun to grow again in her liver, infiltrating nearly all the organs and implacably resistant to any but the most extreme treatment. Kathy Grant, a doctor Barbara chose because of the attention and meticulous care of her initial examination, didn't even examine her this time. The precise dimensions of her liver enlargement no longer matter. The disease process has taken over and now has its own life, past the reach of medical intervention.

A few months left. Ninety days. Perhaps two hundred days. Probably not. When we left the doctor's office, Barbara said she felt trapped in her body and feared she would feel trapped in our home if we went directly there. "Could we take a walk on the beach first?" she asked. As we were driving toward the ocean, she abruptly changed her mind and had me stop at a nearby luncheonette where we sat on stools at the counter. She ordered a patty melt and watched the counterman negotiate his split-second dance. Her father had owned a luncheonette when she was a child, and she used to watch him prepare food. No motion wasted, each move purposeful. Not for her today the gourmet restaurants in which she usually takes such delight. Not for her today an elegant and subdued environment. Today she needed to remember her father behind the counter in her childhood luncheonette.

Sandy
December 20

Barbara and I went with Judy to see the AIDS Quilt now being displayed in the convention center. The entire hall was filled with panels, each lovingly sewn by a partner, friend, or family member of a person who has died of AIDS. There were occasional sounds: of bells, of the tender drone of the names of the dead being read over a loudspeaker, of the muffled sobbing of a man kneeling at his lover's panel. Mostly though, the vast hall was silent as men and women moved slowly, solemnly, on the canvas that created a walkway through the room.

Each panel was quite different from those surrounding it. Some were elaborately designed with objects from the deceased's too-short life; some a simple declaration of name, dates of birth and death; while others were playful, whimsical, and affirming. Each was a tribute to the particularity and unique dimensions of a life that had been lost in this epidemic.

Later, at lunch, I asked Barbara what sort of panel she would have wanted for herself. "A window," she said. "A window to show I wasn't a monad. A window to see out of and to allow others to see into. I would want all my friends to sign it so it would reflect the connectedness of my life. Then I would want it to have a message from you. Something about us. Maybe, 'Can I meet you at the kitchen table?'"

I laughed, remembering how, after all these years, we still used those exact words to announce something important had to be discussed. We would move to the table, put on the kettle for tea, and sit in our usual chairs, waiting for the words—the words that had always connected us. Now, silent, we reached for each other's hands, holding on.

Sandy
December 22

Today is the last day of *Chanukah*, the festival of light, and the winter solstice. It is the day of the longest darkness and the return of the light. Marcia lit the candles as she sang the prayer in Hebrew. The living room filled with light from the *menorah* and in my despair, I felt the comfort and continuity of this ancient ritual.

Sandy
December 26

It has been a few days now. A few days in which I am learning how it feels to have time so compressed, when everything is so heightened. I spend many hours each day on the telephone telling Barbara's close friends of this final change in her illness. This is another of Barbara's ways of protecting those she loves, giving them time to hear and process this devastating news. It is reminiscent of the first time, nearly three years ago, when I had to tell friends, again and again, of her diagnosis of breast cancer. I remember how there were medical questions from some, psychological questions from others, silence and tears from yet others. But in the telling, I came to incorporate the news more and more deeply myself. It is like that now. We are in a different kind of time. A time of collapsed years, plans, dreams, expectations. A time of good-byes, of finishing relationships that are incomplete, a time of opening to each moment.

Janaea flew out for a last visit with Barbara. I have a picture of them smiling on the gray leather sofa, fists raised in a gesture of resistance. They talked easily together about my life after Barbara's death, about Jan's career plans and her future. After a few days, the three of us drove down to Monterey with Valerie and Helen, who are leaving for a six-month sabbatical. We went through the new aquarium. Barbara, as always, was filled with her irrepressible wellspring of enthusiasm for the fish, the coral, for life.

On our last night together, Barbara was very moved as Helen and Valerie told her how much they will miss her, how much they love her, and how sad they are to be going away knowing she will not be here when they return.

Now my youngest daughter, Alison, is here. Her concern about the things of ordinary, daily life, her delight in a publication, all seem beyond the place I am living in. Yet it is the stuff of life. The stuff of her life. She and Barbara sit in the garden talking about ways to shape her dissertation, the pros and cons of academic work. I learn later that Barbara shared her concerns about me and how she hopes both Alison and Janaea will care for me after her death. I'm hugely grateful for my brave and loving daughters and appreciate the continuity they represent in my life.

We attended a large dinner party given by Mark and Lauren on Christmas Day. They prepared a superb and loving meal, surrounded us with witty and interesting people, and created a last celebration filled with effusive, deeply felt tenderness.

Today another leave-taking. Hugh, an old friend, is moving away. Deborah, a colleague from graduate school, flew out to say good-bye. Yesterday Barbara paid a last visit to an old lover. Rachel sat with her in the garden. Then Anna. She reminisced with Francesca propped up in bed. And Gail, who has been here through everything. Cheerful, present, steady. Ruth will arrive soon. And then, finally, her parents. There will always be others with us now. I need to let go of the primacy of our time together, play a more tangential role now, helping her say her good-byes, helping her finish her work here. That is the form of my respect and friendship now. My lonely expression of love.

Barbara
December 30

During the last three months, I have reviewed much of my adult life, returned to those places that were significant to me: North-western University, where I got my Ph.D.; London, where I fell in love with the possibility of a new self. I always go back to New York. It is in my cells as much as the cancer is. You can take the girl out of New York, as the old saying goes, but you can't take New York out of the girl. They can't take the cancer out of me either.

I have seen all my lovers, have spent time with them, remembering the past. I have allowed the sense of each specific love to fill me, so that I could savor it, analyze it, understand it, and cradle it until it yielded its secret to me. Why did I love this person? What was it about me, about him, about her, about that time, that filled me with passion, that ruptured me into love?

In the last months, I have made myself into a goose stuffed for foie gras. I have chained myself in a relentless effort to compress, encapsulate, and fully see the past in rapid reverse. I have stuffed people, places, and events down my throat in an effort to digest them, to distill their essential meanings. Like Odysseus who tied himself to his ship's mast to resist the Sirens, I have chained myself to the truth of my journey backward in order to go forward. I have understood how I have lived and who I am. I feel the thrill of my self and the weariness of the struggle. I am not lonely—not orphaned—not abandoned. I am clean, clear, real. I have arrived here in this moment of my living and my dying.

Barbara's letter
January 1

Dear Friends,

Because of the changes in my health, Sandy and I have altered the focus of our January anniversary ritual.

Our plan now is to share some of our own thoughts and feelings with you. In return we would like each of you to share a memory, a thought, a story, or some favorite moment you think of in connection with me.

This ritual is to mark the moment of passage into a sacred and extraordinary time. This ritual is not a substitute for individual time that I will spend with each one of you. Rather it is a special time we will all spend together in community.

Please come at six-thirty. The ritual will begin at seven-thirty with the ringing of bells. Light refreshments will be served.

Love,

Barbara

Barbara
January 4

There are two reasons for your coming here tonight. First it is the anniversary of the ceremony of commitment you shared with us last year. Second I am entering a sacred time. A time in which there is no way to predict, no knowledge that can be called upon. While I feel cheated because I will die so young, that feeling is counteracted with a feeling of fullness: fullness with my friends, with our community, and with Sandy. As many of you know, I have been writing letters to my nephew, Asher. Letters to be given to him each year on his birthday. Letters that mark my legacy to him. One of those letters is on fullness. I want to read a passage from that letter now.

Dear Asher,

This letter is about the feeling of fullness. It is an extremely important concept to me and one that I think is essential for a good life. It is important because, in my life, I have been a person who has often felt empty. And because of my personal experience with the feeling of emptiness, I have come to understand that the feeling of fullness is one of the most blessed, most unacknowledged, and most underrated feelings I know. I do not mean happiness, nor do I mean contentment, nor do I mean peacefulness. I mean, very simply, that you feel there is enough inside you, that you feel internally rich and varied, that there are no big empty spaces, no holes that gnaw at the fabric of your being. I am also talking about the size human being you experience yourself to be: large or small; generous and expansive, or tight and pinched and hoarding.

Fullness has many meanings. It may mean that you have enough of an inner sense of self to feel that the space within you can be filled up. It may mean your ability to take experiences and turn them into gratifications. There is another meaning of the word fullness that I wish for you and this has to do with the enlargement of your own feeling and perception. I believe that a feeling of fullness arises from the mind's ability to see, notice, and make discriminations between and within categories of things, persons, and events. To put this assumption very simply: the more you can see, the richer your life will be, the more diverse your experience, and therefore, the fuller you can be.

The finer the discriminations one can make, the more precise the perceptions, the more vivid the details, the tinier each piece of information is, the fuller and richer will be the picture you have. Each detail is a particular slice of information, each is to be observed and to be savored. The smaller your discriminations, the richer is your picture of the world and, in turn, the richer your internal life. Your internal landscape may be filled with more units of perception and concentration than perhaps you will know what to do with. Let it be. May you be blessed with an enlarged capacity to discern.

Imagine the depth and breadth of your ability to become more human as you begin to recognize and identify the different types of human experience. Your ability to grow, change, and develop will depend on how much you can discriminate and then empathize with different kinds of human experience.

Let us take, for example, different types of human pain. There is grief. There is sorrow. There is loss. There is disappointment. The more you can tell the difference between each one of these experiences, and the more you can understand each one in its particularity, the more human and alive you can become. The world will be a more complex place and it is within complexity that you can locate richness and diversity of experience.

And, finally, there can be no richness and sense of fullness without others. We take others within our selves, into our souls, to inhabit us and live with us for a while, sometimes even a lifetime. May these occupants of your soul, these introjects, these ghosts, these ancestors, these tenants be benevolent and kind, generous and loving. May you live in common cause with them, not in struggle and conflict. May they illuminate you from inside, letting light shine through you. May you have the generosity of spirit to let them sing through you. May you be expansive enough to surrender part of yourself, to allow yourself to be a vessel for these ancient voices, these ancient truths, these cries filled with mystery and nobility that may possess you in the most unexpected moments.

I wish for you that most of your emptinesses are fillable. I wish for you that you can live with some degree of emptiness, allowing it its own space, allowing it to be the spacious and merciful quiet that it can be. May you not rush to fill it with noise and cheap affections.

As paradoxical as it all sounds, may you be the empty vessel of active agency so that you can have a full and rich life. There is nothing better. Take this from me on faith. I know. I have it and I grieve to lose it.

Love,
Aunt Barbara

Sandy
January 4

The gathered women were silent after Barbara finished reading and leaned back on the sofa, tired now. First one woman spoke, then another, the sounds of their voices picking up speed until we were laughing, crying, remembering together. Stories about a first meeting with Barbara. Memories of outrageous adventures together. Reflections about the meanings of relationship. It was a farewell to Barbara by our community, in community. And a thank-you.

LIVING IN SACRED TIME

JANUARY 1988

Sandy
January 10

The next stage of dying has begun. Last week Barbara decided, after extensive research, not to take any further treatment. The risks of losing quality time because of the side effects of a bone marrow harvest were too great to balance the statistically equivocal benefits.

Last Sunday morning we were in Napa Valley with Jane and Linda eating a breakfast of pancakes and bacon and preparing to see *The Last Emperor*. This Sunday Barbara lies in bed fully clothed, dozing on and off all day. Only one week has made such a marked difference in her strength, appetite, and enthusiasms.

Last night she had pain significant enough to require painkillers every two hours. Sometimes I held her, but at others, even my touch was irritating and we simply held hands until the pills took effect. We talked, as we so often do now, about this book, about ways to shape and complete it. About what direction I will take next in my life. It was calm and loving, and we lay beside each other crying quietly.

This no longer feels like a time of wrenching grief or bitter loss as earlier periods have.

Cheri told me last week that my world would get smaller and smaller. She's right. Smaller and smaller until it will shrink down to just Barbara and me in our bed, curled around each other whispering as we have so many thousands of nights. Whispering about the future, the plans, the dreams. Only now, the dreams and plans are mine.

Sandy

January 12

We went to see Kathy Grant about the pain that Barbara has begun to experience. Barbara asked only if her pain would be episodic or was it a part of the beginning of constant deterioration as the cancer continues to spread. It would be episodic, the doctor replied, explaining the physiology of the source of pain. But this time Barbara didn't counter with her usual barrage of questions. I expected her to ask, "Is this internal bleeding? How frequent is episodic? What should I anticipate next?" But she asked nothing and in a relieved and unnaturally accepting way thanked the doctor as we left. I was uncomfortable with her out-of-character lack of engagement, but when we returned home, Barbara was calm and gazed out of the window into her garden, looking very peaceful.

Sandy

January 23

Ruth came for a few days. It was a warm and loving time for them. But there was a moment, as they sat together at the kitchen table telling stories about being children together, daughters of their parents, siblings with a five-year age difference, that I found myself yearning for a sibling with whom I could share my history, share the precious, unique, private experience of childhood, share this experience of loss. I felt desolate as I sat between them, listening to their words, watching the glances exchanged, the private jokes, the emotional shorthand. I wondered about Janaea and Alison and what they will, or perhaps already do, say at the kitchen tables of their own lives. What was it like for them to have me as a mother? What stories do they tell? How lucky they are to have each other.

Now Barbara has begun studying with our rabbi. While I manage to keep balance most of the time, I feel myself in a kind of futureless limbo. Each moment has such immediacy that I cannot focus on anything that is outside the narrowing perimeters of our life together. I cannot spend time at my office without becoming fidgety and anxious to return home. I need to be here, somewhere in the house. It isn't necessary that I interact with Barbara. I just need to know that she is down the hall, sleeping in the next room, talking on the phone, visiting with a friend in the kitchen, or sitting in the garden she so lovingly planted. Then I can steady myself.

Our nights are longer now. Barbara often awakens, breathing with difficulty. She tries not to take pain medication without first trying to relax as I read from the sheet of meditations Ruth left me. Sometimes the drone of my words or my hand on the small of her back making widening circles soothes her and she can return to sleep. At other times nothing allays the anxiety and pain and I get up, turn on the light, and get the pain medication and anti-nausea pill that must accompany it.

Our private life is in the night now. Our days are filled with phone calls and people eager to be allowed to help. They cook, walk the dog, visit—anything that will make them feel useful and help us to negotiate the day. Barbara is very internal now and her attention is focused on writing a series of thirteen letters to her nephew, Asher. Each essay examines a dimension of living ethically and morally. I am to give him one for each birthday and have them bound as her gift to him at the time of his *bar mitzvah*. She writes of courage, honor, passion, love. They are inscribed to Asher, but are also for Ruth and for me. Part of her legacy to us.

She goes to the typewriter upon awakening and begins to type feverishly, wanting to get everything down on the page before her energy begins to wane. We go for walks less often now, her strength so unpredictable and limited. Sometimes we will go to a gallery or a cafe for her much-loved *caffe latté*, or just for the stimulation of a different neighborhood. The wheelchair I insisted upon ordering sits unopened and unused in her study. I imagine she is getting used to its presence in her own way. She says nothing about using it. There will be time enough for a wheelchair, I suppose. I hope.

Sandy
January 25

At their first meeting, nearly six weeks ago, Barbara told Rabbi Kahn about the love of learning in her family and defined herself as a "cultural" Jew. But now, she told him, she had discovered a wish to study, to prepare for her death in traditional ways, and was unsure about how to proceed through this new and unexpected set of feelings. Knowing Barbara's modesty, I described the series of thirteen letters she was writing to Asher. The rabbi told her that what she was doing had a long and significant history. She was writing an ethical will. He gave her a book that described the history of ethical wills during the Middle Ages and they shook hands, making an appointment to meet the following week.

When we left the synagogue, I asked her if she was sorry we had never gone to Friday night services all those weeks and months we had meant to. Softly she answered, "No. It's not the community I long for. We have community. It's the contact with a learned and gentle man."

Now in her weekly appointments with the rabbi she reads about ethical wills, Jewish mourning rituals, cremation, and *midrash*. It is a startling return to a history that was always ambivalently handled by her parents, more cultural and political Jews than religious ones. But the teachings give her comfort now, a sense of place and of time, and an ability to see herself on a continuum between life and death, between the past and the future, between her beloved grandmother, dead now for decades, and her two-year-old nephew, Asher.

Sandy
January 27

I sit in a small anteroom, outside the *mikvah*. Barbara is taking a ritual bath to mark the "separation" between one state of being and another. It is the same ritual she watched Barbara Myerhoff take, the symbolic act of re-entering the womb by being totally immersed in water, then emerging reborn, ready to re-unite with God. While this is a monthly ritual for orthodox Jewish women, the *mikvah* taken in preparation for death is considered the holiest of all and Barbara has been very solemn in her preparations. "People are pulling me back," she said last night at dinner. "They are pulling me back into their need for me, their need for me not to die, into our shared history. I need now to move forward and mark this time with my writing, my preparations, my being present in each moment."

Barbara
January 28

There are a lot of lessons that come with this disease, or maybe it's just that you learn to make them into lessons. I am a very different person now: more open, much more righteous, much more honest, and more self-knowing. After getting cancer I saw that being a sociologist was just the smallest part of who I am. There are so many riches, so many interests, so many other parts of myself. Instead of losing myself, instead of being consumed by this disease—and it can consume you if you don't watch it—instead, I grew. I turned it into a possibility for opening up to myself, for discovering, and for exploring new areas.

I've realized that I want to list the ways in which cancer can do that. You can get courage to take larger risks than you ever have before. I mean, you're already sick, so what can happen to you? You can have much more courage in saying things and in living than you ever had before. That's the first thing I think about, that cancer has released the courage in me.

And you can do things you've always wanted to do. Cancer, by giving you the sense of your own mortality, can entice you into doing those things you have been postponing. You do it today, and you do it now. Cancer actualizes you in that way, by not waiting. It reduces the conflicts you have about things—you just do them. You don't postpone anymore.

You have this sense of urgency. And you can turn this urgency— you can harness this energy that propels you—so that you go ahead and do these things and discover new parts of yourself. *All* the things you ever wanted to do, *all* the dreams you had. And the dreams that you couldn't even dream, because you didn't allow yourself. God, if you can't do anything else, at least have the dream! At least know your dream.

Cancer has put me in touch with that. And then also, it has taught me to enjoy the tenderness and the preciousness of every moment. Moments are very important because there may not be any after that—or you may throw up. Cancer exquisitely places you in the moment.

I have become very human to myself in a way that I would never have imagined. I've become a bigger person, a fuller person. This to me is one of the greatest lessons: just being human. Having cancer doesn't mean that you lose yourself at all. For me it meant that I discovered myself.

Sandy

January 29

She is failing quickly. Today is Friday. I look back at my datebook and see that three weeks ago we went to Berkeley to have dinner with friends. The following Friday we lit the Sabbath candles with Ruth. Last Friday Cheri came to dinner. Now Barbara stays in bed resting and sleeping. Her appetite is greatly diminished and she is unable to enjoy the gourmet meals she so loved. Only yogurt and custard now. Her parents are here and struggle to stay strong, supportive, helpful. I see them as they look at her, feel the pause before they ask her if she wants tea, juice, an apple, anything? I try to make them feel useful, leaving kitchen tasks for them so they don't feel displaced.

Barbara has pulled more within herself. After all these years, her lifetime, in fact, of painstakingly protecting her parents, she scarcely interacts with them. "I don't have emotions like you do anymore," she whispers to me.

In the night she murmurs, "I hope you will let our friends hold and comfort you."

"I will," I promise, beginning to weep. She reaches for my hand, kisses each of my fingers, her body too sore now to nestle against mine.

Barbara
January 29

It is 2 a.m., I've just taken two narcotic painkiller pills. The pain in my liver aches and the meds don't hold well in the night.

I'm dying. I'm going to die. I have about a month left. And if I can write for the next two weeks, I'll be grateful. Fuck that shit! Up until the very last day! The writing is at least as deep and cellular as the cancer. And here is a journal entry at 2 a.m. Lonely, quiet, I can't make this intense loneliness and fear go away. Narcotics help. They dull everything a little bit, but the tragedy center of my brain is barely touched by any pill. For that, two stiff martinis and a good cry.

Jewish food and stories: my parents are here watching their daughter die. They are fiercely strong and tenacious, complying with my wishes to hide their grief, share it with my sister and Sandy but to be strong and positive with me. How right I was all along to spare them three years of anguish that would have diminished otherwise especially sweet and delicious years.

Barbara
January 30

I don't want this time to evaporate because I haven't thought about how I want to spend it. I have been a fighter all my life. Things have not come easily to me, and despite the years of what felt like an ongoing battle with the world to get what I wanted, I never developed the calluses that strategizing, manipulating, and cajoling might confer. My mother always said that I was too honest, too straightforward, without one bone in my body that knew how to make things easier without having it feel manipulative. I come to this place with honesty and few defenses. Since I worked so hard in my life, this will be a time that I will take easily and gently. I will not fight hard or endure inhumane treatments whose benefits are equivocal. I will not fight loudly into the night. I will go softly and with love.

Barbara's letter to friends
February 1

Dear Friends,

The chemotherapy is no longer working and the cancer in my liver is growing again. My doctor told me about one medical option, but after looking up the statistics, I decided against it. It has terrible side effects, great risks, and few rewards. Now medicine has no more knowledge to offer me. So I have decided to face this period with the wisdom that love and friendship provide and use the time I have left to write and to have fun.

I feel as if I have entered a sacred period because there is no knowledge, only faith and hope. Because I see this as a sacred time, I have arranged to study with Rabbi Yoel Kahn of Temple Sha'ar Zahav. We talk about such things as burial versus cremation and the meanings of scripture and the commentaries. I have also recently engaged in a transformative experience known as *mikvah*, which consists of a ritual bath. It is usually used for entering holiness or union with God. I have discovered that I am a woman of deep faith and am moved by the teachings. One friend, from the Quaker tradition, tells me she holds me in the Light. Another friend, a former priest, tells me we'll meet in a better place. I respond to all their images and metaphors and see commonality among them. But I respond most to very specifically Jewish images and cultural themes, such as music, food, language, and my religious heritage.

Therefore, this is my last letter to you. It's not because I am very sick (although I'm having symptoms at this time) but because I am studying Torah and because I'm writing. I have entered an inward period; contact with people and interaction are difficult for me and I must follow that impulse very seriously.

I think that I have finished most of my business and have already said proper good-byes to most of you. If there is something you'd like to tell me, please write me a letter. I cannot be sure I will answer it but you can count on the fact that I'll read it.

I have been thinking how fortunate I have been to live through a period of history that was perhaps one of the most idealistic and energetic times in America in this century. My first memory is the night World War II ended, when there were parties in the streets of Brooklyn and I was allowed to stay up late and eat ice cream.

My memories of public school are filled with hula hoops and Davy Crockett songs. In my early teens, there was lots of rock and roll by groups called the Cadillacs and the Orioles. Sha Boom. Earth Angel. Get a Job. At fifteen and sixteen, I danced on television on the Alan Freed after-school rock and roll show. My high school and college days were filled with movies by Fellini, Antonioni, Bergman, and Godard. I remember when seeing a movie like *Hiroshima, Mon Amour* was the equivalent of reading a great book.

I dropped out of Brooklyn College after one year to leave home, move to the East Village, and live the life of a bohemian. In 1963 and 1964, I spent my time doing volunteer work at the CORE office in Manhattan, answering telephones, raising funds, licking envelopes. In 1965 I was organizing rent strikes on 85th and Columbus Avenue, then regarded as the worst blocks in Manhattan. Now you can't even get a condo in that neighborhood.

I vividly remember the day Goodman, Schwerner and Chaney were killed, and later Viola Liuzzo, the civil rights worker from Detroit. I remember the marches and the songs. And then there were marches and songs against Vietnam. Songs by Joan Baez and Phil Ochs, burning draft cards, organizing on campus, first at Brooklyn College and then at Northwestern University. I remember with great fondness being part of a group that took over the administrative office at Brooklyn College. Fellow students jeered at us, cops came and told us to get out before the arrests would begin. I got out and went home, only to see pictures of my boyfriend on television, being beaten by the police. I remember when Martin Luther King was shot. And soon after that, the day Robert Kennedy was shot and how I couldn't sleep for days.

The summer of 1969 was the summer of Woodstock but I wasn't there. I was in San Francisco getting my life together, deciding I would go to graduate school in the Midwest after all. It never occurred to me that I would be utterly transformed. I remember graduate school as one of the grandest times of my life, full of rebellion and idealism. There was the "greening of America" and "tuning in, turning on and tuning out." It was the place of great intellectual explosion and wonderful friends and deep connections, friendships that have lasted a lifetime.

At Northwestern University, I went on protest marches sandwiched in between classes. It began with a protest against the assassination of Fred Hampton and other Black Panthers in Chicago. Then there was the bombing of Cambodia, Kent State, and the closing of campuses all over the country. And then there were the meetings and all-night discussions and the all-female collectives that soon would be labeled the "women's liberation movement."

I remember Janis and Jimi, when each of them died; I remember, ten years before, Chubby Checker and the Peppermint Lounge, Elvis Presley, and Eldridge Cleaver. George Jackson and Angela Davis. And the Beatles.

Then there were the years at Stanford where I had the opportunity to work with good minds and well-educated kids. I learned how to become a good teacher. And I learned how to don the identity of a professional sociologist. I did a 180 degree turn in my next job, which was with an Adult Masters Program at Vermont College in San Francisco. There I learned about living a full intellectual life. I became engaged in a daily practice in which my political and ethical concerns became integrated with my professional identity. It is, of course, predictable that living a fuller life also means that one's professional life is more rewarding. That's what happened to me at Vermont College. I found my *metier*. I found myself, and my professional life as a sociologist improved too. Everything improved.

That wasn't the only 180 degree turn I made. I went from an eight-year relationship with a man to a long-term relationship with a woman. Sandy and I have been partners since 1979 and this relationship is one of the great accomplishments of my life. It was a crucible in which we found ourselves able to grow and change, able to find new and healthy ways of loving, able to find satisfactions and continuities that had eluded each of us before. We are work partners, roommates, confidants, friends, and lovers. We have written together and we continue writing together. We have become whole people because of one another. I am extraordinarily fortunate to have had this wonderful relationship, this wonderful person, Sandy, in my life.

As I reread this, I seem to have left out so much. It is a political history, of course, but I neglected to write of my aesthetic tastes. I remember my parents taking me to the Brooklyn Museum and the Brooklyn Botanic Gardens at least five times a year when I was small. I went through periods of preference, liking the French Impressionists first, then Picasso and other moderns in my twenties, then the New York abstract expressionists who remain my favorites.

As my tastes grew, I learned to love '20s and '30s engravings of city skylines and subway trains, textiles and calligraphy, naif art, and botanical engravings.

Music, too, was always a big part of my life. At nineteen I studied classical guitar. I loved form and pure line and was always attracted to Bach. But as I grew older, my tastes incorporated Gershwin, Milhaud, Villa-Lobos, Stravinsky, Poulenc. I always loved jazzy ragtime themes as they were worked into classical compositions. But in this last year of my life, I have come to love Schubert and Brahms because they touch my heart in a way other composers cannot reach. It is often difficult for me to hear their music, especially during this period. It goes to the deepest, most heartbreaking places in my soul and sometimes I can't stand being opened to that level of sensitivity in myself.

Gardening has also been an important part of my life. For a girl who grew up in the projects of Brooklyn, I've turned into quite a farmer. For years I grew vegetables in my 10' x 10' garden using all kinds of methods. I composted. I used the French intensive method. My yields were huge, my tomatoes delicious, and my little garden buzzed with earthworms and other insect life. When I met Sandy, I switched from vegetables to flowers exclusively. Sandy's greatest desire was to fill our home with fresh flowers every Monday morning and have each room be bright and alive with color. I was determined to give her that. I grew irises, orchids, and hundreds of different bulbs. Here in San Francisco, we were blessed with two bloomings a year. I joined the Horticultural Society and began to specialize in orchids and bromeliads, both of which have ordinary leaves but unexpectedly luminous spikes of extraordinary color and shape.

Reading has always been one of the central activities of my life. My room is filled with books from floor to ceiling. I got my first public library card at eight. I tip-toed into the adult reading room and never stopped. As a first-year graduate student, I read eight years worth of every monthly publication of the major journals in my field. I read to learn the history of my discipline and where I fit into it. As a sociologist I have served many times in an editorial capacity on professional journals, as well as serving on committees that selected the best work of sociology published that year. Professional involvements that combine literary and sociological acumen are a source of much pride to me. I am grateful for the capacity to be fed by a diet with such variations.

Finally my own writing has been a source of joy and nourishment for me. I learned how to become a writer, not just a sociologist using the scaffolding of data to tell a story. I write because I'm a human being who has learned how to describe the inner landscape. Now Sandy and I are completing a book that traces the journey of my cancer. It is called *Cancer in Two Voices*. Even though I may not see the bound volume in my lifetime, I know that the book is already useful because published excerpts have received appreciative responses.

It was a good life. It was a wonderful life and each of you who reads this is part of the fabric that made it wonderful, whole, and meaningful. I go in peace and calm. I shall miss you.

Love,

Barbara

THE LAST SABBATH

FEBRUARY 1988

Sandy
February 4

In December Barbara met with Rabbi Kahn every Monday morning. I drove her to the synagogue where she would eagerly climb the steep flight of stairs to his office. When I returned an hour later, her face would be shining, animated, as she described their discussions. Interpretations of the Book of Jonah. The history of ethical wills. The post-Holocaust view of cremation. Her mind raced to keep up with this scholarly teacher. But the inevitable Monday in January arrived when she was too weak to dress, to climb the stairs to his office, to reason and spar, to struggle with ideas. Instead the rabbi agreed to come to our home to continue their ongoing dialogue. Welcoming him, then serving tea, I prepared to absent myself during their meeting and was surprised when Barbara asked me to join them. As I sat uncertainly on the sofa beside her, she straightened up with some effort, looked squarely at the rabbi, and announced, "Today we need to plan my funeral."

Having officiated at the funerals of many gay men and lesbians, he began by suggesting some words by Stephen Spender and the poetry of Adrienne Rich. Barbara cut him off in mid-sentence, saying firmly, "No. That's not what I want. This service is for my parents. They don't know who Adrienne Rich is or what Stephen Spender wrote. They won't understand or be comforted with the poetry of strangers. They need the ancient words, the prayers, the sounds."

Rabbi Kahn heard the intensity in her voice, nodded, and took out a small pad to make notes on this last rite of passage. The last offering of love to her parents.

They began again, this time more slowly, with less certainty. Barbara wanted her ethical will, her letters to Asher, to be a part of her funeral service. She asked the rabbi to read from the letter in which she wrote of the importance of having a social dream, a letter that honored the lives of her parents. Their lives had been ones of walking precincts, organizing door to door, marching in demonstrations—leaving a legacy of what she called their "gentle brand of Brooklynese socialism." In this letter, she wrote, "The major reason I became a teacher was to inject my students with the passion of a social dream. I believe strongly that knowledge is power and I wanted to be an agent of transmission of knowledge. I wanted my students to have hope, to have the energy to fight good struggles, and I wanted to pass my dream on to hundreds of people I could influence."

As their discussion continued and our pads filled with suggested readings and prayers, I turned to Barbara and blurted, "I want to speak too. I need to have my words a part of the service."

"Of course, love," she whispered, squeezing my hand weakly. "It couldn't be any other way. Your words are a part of everything." Flashing me a teasing smile, her energy visibly faded, she excused herself to return to bed where she now spent most of her time. I led the rabbi down the long hallway, my eyes burning with tears.

"Thank you," I murmured as I opened the front door. "Thank you for being so responsive, so gentle, so present."

Our eyes held each other for a brief moment; then he moved down the front stairs and I returned to the rocking chair beside our bed. It had been positioned there for the past month so that Barbara could see me when she woke from sleep, so that I could sit and read to her, write with her, be close by.

Barbara

February 7

I am now dying. There is no treatment for me anymore. In the future there will be other kinds of drugs called biological enhancers, drugs like interferon and interleukin, that stimulate the immune system to fight the cancer. Doctors will be able to offer newer treatments with fewer side effects. But it is not the future yet.

Nor is it the past. But I sit, remembering my younger self, camera hanging from my shoulder, darkroom in the basement, images and their meanings a consuming interest. Now I wonder what a series of photographs representing my dying would look like. How would I photograph myself now?

I try to imagine a series of pictures of me taken at 9 a.m. Three months ago they would have shown a bright, spunky woman walking her dog or eating a big breakfast of ham and eggs, complete with cups of steaming coffee made from first-class beans ground only moments before filtering. Or perhaps the pictures would show me sitting at the typewriter, looking intense and full of concentration, pounding energetically, trying in a last-minute attempt to fix the words to the page.

Three weeks later the 9 a.m. pictures would be different. Breakfast is a small bowl of porridge and I may be sitting at the table in my bathrobe rather than in my daily clothing. There would be no more pictures of me walking the pooch. I now pace around the apartment. It's safer and when my breath runs out, I lie down until I can catch my breath once again. The hilly, slanted streets of San Francisco, the ones that look so good in chase scenes in Hollywood movies, are too hard for me now. But there's still a picture of me sitting at the typewriter.

Another three weeks pass. The 9 a.m. images are different yet again. I sit at the table in my bathrobe, staring at the glass of orange juice and the anti-nausea pill. The next image shows me struggling to get it down. By now I hardly walk around the apartment. Even that is too tiring. Staying in bed is simpler and I can breathe more easily by lying flat, so that my swollen liver does not push against my diaphragm, thereby decreasing the amount of air I can inhale. The swelling in my abdomen is now visible. I look pregnant but am merely filled with fluids that no longer pass into the liver, but rather collect stagnantly in the abdominal tissues. This is the first visible sign of my illness. All the other images have merely shown differences in my behavior. There are no more pictures of me at the typewriter. Instead I write in bed on the lap desk given to me by a friend.

Three weeks later I'm sleeping at 9 a.m. If the film were color, it would show a yellow tone to my skin and eyes. Liver malfunction manifests itself as jaundice. In one picture my left eyelid is lifted slightly, a sign that I understand that I am being photographed, but that I am too weak to speak or interact or perhaps even to care. I am forty-four years old.

Sandy
February 14

VALENTINE'S DAY. Barbara died today.

Sandy
February 15

You lay on your bed, three days ago, swollen with edema, watching the doctor. "You have a few weeks at most," she said, an unexpected gift from this brusque woman.

The next day your bloated, swollen body was unable to turn, to move, to walk. The mouth sores made speech uncomfortable. Reduced now from sentences to words, from glasses of ice water to a child's bottle, your hand too weak to hold the glass. "I think it's time," you whispered to me.

I stroked your leg that was bent towards me, towards contact. It was the only part of your body I could touch or caress without causing you discomfort, the only way I could soothe your sore, sweet flesh. I whispered again, as I had so many times in the past year, that I would be at your side when your death came. With that reassurance you drifted back to sleep and I knew with mournful clarity that this might be one of the last nights I would ever lie beside you, hear your breath rise and fall, stroke your leg, place my lips on your shoulder, your ear, your arm. I remained awake beside you all through the rest of that night. Loving you.

At exactly eleven-fifteen the next morning, Valentine's Day, you sent me into the kitchen for some fresh water, smiling up at me with love. When I re-entered our room, just moments later, with herb tea and ice water, you were already dead. Your eyes open, your body open, your lips soft and parted. After calling out to Ruth and Stan, I lay down beside you, gathered you into my arms, and began to speak.

"I love you. Go gently towards the light my dearest love. Go with love and with calm. *S'hma Yisroel Adonai Elohenu Adonei Echod.* Go peacefully toward the light my love," I murmured.

My hand rested on your narrow chest, circling your heart. My hand on your heart where it had been a year before as we stood together under the *chupah.* Now, again, for the last time, my hand on your heart, my words becoming sighs. I dimly heard Ruth singing traditional Yiddish songs from your shared childhood, felt Stan take your hand in his, felt us join in this moment, fused around your body. Our beloved Barbara.

Some minutes later Ruth and Stan left the bedroom to comfort each other and I cradled you, able now to hold your limp body without pain. Needing to make an imprint on my palms, I ran my hands along your familiar shape, kissed you to remind my lips of your taste, your smell. Memories to carry with me for my life.

"Good-bye my dearest love. Thank you for loving me so deeply and so well. I will keep you in my heart for as long as I live. You fill and nourish me now as you did in life. I am blessed with you. May you travel with mercy and with light. Amen."

Sandy
February 16

Barbara's body is again dressed in the clothes she wore at our ceremony of commitment thirteen months ago, a day she said was the happiest of her life. Rabbi Kahn mounted the *bema* to speak the words they had decided upon, the readings they had chosen together, to lead the service she had wanted. The cantor sang the traditional songs as her parents sat beside me, dazed, the traditional black ribbon cut almost in two, symbolizing the rending of their hearts, a slash upon their chests.

Midway through the service, the rabbi paused and nodded to me. I rose to the *bema*, looked down at the redwood coffin with a Star of David carved upon it, and spoke.

"I awoke early this morning and sat on the window seat overlooking Barbara's garden, trying to listen to the words she might have me say. 'How do I say good-bye to you?' I asked her. 'Of all the words I might choose, which ones are fitting and loving for such a task?'

"I sat for a while and began to understand that my eyes will no longer be able to look upon her; my arms will no longer hold her; my voice will no longer meet hers in tuneless song; my words no longer have the benefit of her acute editorial skill. Our talking and talking and talking at the kitchen table about everything—our minds eagerly racing to meet each other—will no longer be a part of my days.

"Still, my heart is filled with her. Today and for a long time to come. It is a heavy heart, filled with my own loss, my own sorrow. But it is also a heart that has been blessed by Barbara, nourished by her, a heart that has fully opened to a deep and an abiding love. That was her gift to me, and I am enriched by it and have taken her into me and into the ways that I will live for all the days of my life."

When I finished, I looked down at the coffin, imagining Barbara inside it in her purple satin blouse and black silk pants. I spoke directly to her. "It truly was a sacred pilgrimage. Thank you, love."

Descending from the pulpit, I moved past her parents, still staring straight ahead, past her sister, Stan, and lowered myself onto the wooden pew. As the rabbi completed the service by leading the mourners in the *Kaddish*, the prayer for the dead, the living disrupted Barbara's carefully arranged offering. The words "*Yit-ga-dal ve-yit-ka-dash she-mei ra-ba*" filled the sanctuary and with them the sound of a shriek, sustained for a heartbeat and becoming a wail, grew higher and louder as Barbara's mother pushed herself out of her seat and began to move toward the coffin containing the body of her first-born. The sound was a barrier, a shield to stop the inexorable process of this prayer, this ending. Her wailing rose above the murmuring of the assembled, gathering force, gathering strength. As her throat pushed forth these primitive sounds, I remembered the sounds of labor and birth, the elemental sounds the body emits when it is beyond its capacity to tolerate pain. Her wails became keening and the keening blurred back into language, pleading. Words she was speaking to Barbara, to God, to anyone who could erase this moment.

"Not my Barbara. Take me. Please take me. I'm old and I'm ready. It's not right. It's not natural. Let me go in her place." Her face contorted as she moved toward her child in a redwood coffin. Words insufficient now, she pressed herself towards her child and began again to wail. She shed no tears but made an agonized sound that was both riveting in its force and horrifying in its anguish.

Ruth rose, now her mother's only daughter, and she and Stan flanked the old couple and ushered them out of the chapel. Regina's body sagged, her cries grew fainter and more desperate as she was led away. As the *Kaddish* ended, the service complete, I rose to greet the mourners and felt, before I saw, my two daughters move to surround me, to flank me in the same way, assuring me of their presence, their breath. These grown women, my children. They stood silently on each side of me, giving continuity, making this moment bearable.

Returning home, the house was already filled with women moving briskly around the kitchen. Traditionally only friends and neighbors can prepare and serve the food during this period, leaving the mourners free to grieve. Coffee was brewed, cakes piled high on platters. A meal of consolation. Ruth led her parents into the living room and Regina lowered herself heavily into my father's old, tufted, leather chair, its high back and sturdy arms dwarfing her, her legs scarcely touching the floor. She had been sedated and responded with a polite blankness to the steady stream of friends who approached her chair with their murmured condolences.

Then Debbie, a friend who is an oncological nurse, placed her hand gently on my arm and said, "What Barbara's mother did was so powerful and important. She remembers how to mourn, how to make the sound we have all forgotten and needed to hear. She is a woman who is not muted and well behaved in her grief as we have learned to be."

In that moment I understood what Barbara had forgotten to include in her planning—the missing link in her loving preparations. She had forgotten the necessity to leave space for the sound of the one who unexpectedly survives again. The sound a mother makes when she must outlive her first-born. And in that moment, the day became whole and intact. The traditional Hebrew prayers. The chanting. The words of a political life. And finally the wailing and shrieking. Let there be gnashing of teeth. Crashes of thunder. Bolts of lightning. The heavens opened and took her first-born child, my love. A proper farewell; the ritual was now complete.

Sandy
February 20

During the week of *shiva*, the period of mourning, the house was always filled with women. Some bustling, relieved to have tasks to occupy them and a concrete way to express their sorrow; others awkward, needing to talk about inconsequential things, unable to meet my eyes; and still others comfortable to sit quietly with me. There was constant movement, although my primary memory is that of sitting in my father's chair, being told to eat, and nodding, trying to pay attention to what was going on around me. Pies, cakes, noodle pudding, briskets, and soups filled the counters and refrigerator. I ate very little and sleep was impossible. I filled my nights prowling in and out of our rooms, lifting and replacing each object: pictures, books, vases, love letters, shopping lists. Each with a specific memory, each evoking her presence. I didn't dream about her, but these objects served to bring her close to me during the night.

Each evening the rabbi and cantor came to the house to lead the prayers and chanting that mark the *shiva* period. I remained poised through it all, suspended, waiting for Friday, the last Sabbath, when I would complete our private ritual: the moment when I would put Barbara's ashes into her garden, that 10' x 10' plot of ground she had tended and nurtured for fifteen years. As I sat on the window seat on Thursday, I saw Bruce and Cameron, our upstairs neighbors, both of whom have AIDS, meticulously and silently preparing the garden for the scattering of Barbara's ashes. I watched gratefully as they pulled weeds, arranged the vines on trellises, raked, watered. An act of recognition for a neighbor, a friend, a comrade in a time of plague.

As the sun set on Friday, February 19, those who had been

invited to join in the ceremony of the last Sabbath gathered in the living room. Stan and I had gone out earlier in the day—the first time I had left the house all week—to drive to the chapel and collect the square, brown plastic box that now held Barbara's ashes. It stood on the glass table as the candles were lit and the Sabbath prayers repeated. With the candles burning, we assembled in Barbara's garden.

Jane rang the same Tibetan bells that had begun our ceremony of commitment. As their clear sound faded, she said, "We've come together as this day turns into night, to enrich this garden with Barbara's spirit and being, with the ashes that represent her own returning to the earth. Each flower that has grown here and will grow here is like her life in many ways: a moment in the great span of time, of colorful, varied beauty, tended carefully with full consciousness.

"Before the ashes are scattered, let us each plant something in the garden in honor of Barbara's life, spirit, and love for growing things."

Each person kneeled then, placed a plant brought especially for this purpose into the ground, patted the soil gently around its roots with words of farewell to Barbara.

Later I was told by Janaea that I looked at everyone and said, "It's time to put my honey into her garden now." Opening the box, I buried my fingers into her ash, her bone, and scooped out handfuls, letting them sift through my fingers and drift down to blanket the soil. Circling the garden three times, being sure her essence covered every inch of the small space, I tenderly completed the cycle of birth, life, and death, and created a rebirth in this small sanctuary.

Sandy
February 21

It is now early morning. I sit alone in Barbara's garden, filled with flowers and a film of gray ash, the ground moist, the birds greeting each other and the new day. I look up into the living room to see the memorial candle burning, the candle that has burned all week, steady, constant, warming.

Barbara insisted on consciousness in everything. She faced her death squarely, honestly, saying everything. She needed to be in our bed, with me, with Stan, with Ruth. Insistent that she take back the control that was wrested from her by the inexorable spread of the disease, the depletion of her strength and energy. She took that control back when she decided not to continue "salvage treatment"—when she weighed the risks against the gains and chose a conscious death.

Now the week of mourning is complete—the ceremonies, the prayers —the public and the private rituals are done. The words have all been said. The white lily that Joyce brought on the morning of Barbara's death has dropped its yellowed petals. The memorial candle will soon burn down and sputter out. Now the blossoming and the flame must be in my conscious life.

Sandy
February 25

My new mourning/morning ritual begins when I awake. My movements are very exact. I rise. Put on water for coffee. Go to the bathroom. Grind the coffee beans. Get dressed in my purple sweats. Open the shades in Barbara's office to let in the early morning light she enjoyed. Pour the hot water through the French roast beans she taught me to love. Bring in the papers (unread now for over two weeks). Drink one cup of coffee as I sit at our kitchen table. Tie on my sneakers. Gather the keys and leave. This all takes perhaps fifteen minutes, but the sharp, wounding memory of her death that is my first thought each morning is blurred by this consistent and predictable pattern.

I drive on the same roads to the same destination each morning, through the clogged rush-hour streets, entering an unexpectedly spacious and open Marina where Sembei begins to wriggle excitedly. I open the car door and she leaps out to race to the track where we walk. I follow and am filled with the rush of cool, moist morning air, the smells of the Bay, the view of the Golden Gate Bridge. I begin to walk. My lungs inhale gulps of clean air. My heart begins to pump more rapidly as I move. I am alive and another day has begun.

When I return home, I prepare myself for the rush of memory

every act dislodges. As I sit at the kitchen table, I can hear Barbara chirp, "What is your day today?" as she settled into her seat, red terry robe wrapped around her. I would outline the calls, errands, correspondence, appointments I had planned. We would discuss and list the ingredients for dinner.

At night we would sit again at the table, leaning towards each other, a pot of freshly brewed tea between us. We would "dish," describing interesting articles, conversations, people we had seen. We would fill the kitchen with our words, our enthusiasms, our delight in one another's lives. I have no one to tell my day to now. The ebb and flow of people through my life remains unsaid. There is a stillness to the evenings as I draw the window shades in her office, take out the papers and sit for a restless moment in her garden, where I feel most alone.

Sandy
February 27

This morning on my way to the Marina, I honked angrily at a slow-moving car. "C'mon," I exploded, "let's go." Startled at hearing my own voice fill the silence of the car, I remembered I wasn't in a hurry. It didn't matter anymore what time I got home, for I no longer could throw open our front door and command Sembei, "Go find Barbara. Go on. Go find Barbara and kiss her." Now, whenever I entered our home, it would be still, no sound of her clacking typewriter, no television playing as she rested in bed, no Bach or the Temptations filling the living room and spilling out into her garden as she planted seeds, bulbs, life.

Sandy
February 28

I awoke early to the sound of a soft rain, the first since her death. I moved to the window seat in the still-darkened living room and looked out at the moist garden, imagined the coarse granules of her ash sliding off the cala leaves and penetrating the soil.

I lowered my hand between my legs, feeling my moistness,

touched myself with the same awesome gentleness with which I had touched her on the day she died.

"We had fun together, didn't we?" you asked each one who had come to say good-bye. "That's what it's all about. Having good times together. Loving each other."

Yes, my dearest Barbara. We loved each other. I shall miss you.

AFTERWORD

AUGUST 1990 – FEBRUARY 1991

August

Thirty months have passed. The apartment is filled with photographs; Barbara's mother has said to me that nothing remains now but this "paper daughter." There is still a bar of English soap in the medicine chest that was last pressed against her body. A well-worn flannel shirt hangs on a hook behind the bedroom door. Her bathrobe with the clown pin on its lapel and the accompanying green loafers are still among my clothes in the closet. I imagine her smell is in them.

A few weeks ago, I cleaned out the linen closet, tearing off the torn and faded shelf paper, thinking back to that afternoon over a decade before: a time when we knelt alongside each other, mouths filled with thumbtacks, Martha and the Vandellas providing accompaniment in the background, lining each shelf with iris-covered paper. Now the shelves are dusty, filled with half-empty bottles of sunscreen and Vaseline. I filled a plastic bag with them, remembering each trip, each sunburn.

My work as the executor of Barbara's financial affairs is finished. All her bills have been paid, gifts given to loved ones, and accounts emptied. The two halves of her credit cards fell away as my scissors bisected them.

I still sleep on her side of the bed to protect myself against the longing that I will awake to see her lying there, smiling a whispered good morning.

I have worked on this manuscript for months that have turned into years—writing, shaping, pruning, deleting repetitions, re-arranging for greater chronological ease, and weeping, as I came to more fully understand my responsibility to complete what we had begun together.

Earlier this year I spent two months at a writers' retreat. My cabin was furnished with a wood-burning stove and each night I watched successive drafts go up in smoke. Each morning I shoveled out the ashes and scattered them on the flower bed outside my cottage.

Several months later Sembei was diagnosed with an advanced cancerous tumor in her throat. She was fourteen years old and unable to tolerate chemotherapy. Sorrowfully I had her put to sleep. "Sembei, go find Barbara. Go find Barbara and kiss her." Then her small body was cremated and a second ceremony held, so that her bone and ash might join Barbara's in the garden.

September 5

Now, during a routine medical exam, a lump has been discovered in my throat, one that after extensive testing is diagnosed as thyroid cancer. As I walked home alone from the endocrinologist's office, I remembered Barbara's crumpled face when, six years before, after rushing home from Winnipeg, I had entered our front hallway, my anger and impotence forming a mixture akin to frenzy. I spread out my arms, she walked into them, and we stood, rocking against each other, small moaning sounds filling the stillness. Now I enter the apartment, wrap my arms around myself, and begin to stride up and down the long hallway. I move, unable to still myself, unable to feel, to believe this thing is happening. Write it down, I think to myself. Do what you have done. It works, I whisper to myself. Record this.

September 11

My cancer was, like Barbara's, asymptomatic. But unlike hers, my cancer was found early because I go every year to a private doctor who has time, is thorough, and has an ongoing medical relationship with me.

Immediately after my diagnosis, a flurry of referrals followed. "Top men," as Barbara's mother would say. Men and women who listen patiently and respectfully to my list of questions carefully itemized on a yellow pad. Pam goes with me as I had gone with Barbara. Another set of ears, another set of questions. An ally.

Each doctor I consult is briskly comforting about my papillary carcinoma. It is completely self-contained, they assure me. So unlike me. So unlike Barbara's aggressive cancer, rapidly spreading through her lymph system, through her body.

September 16

Within a few days will be the start of the Days of Awe, beginning with *Rosh Hashanah*, marking the beginning of the Jewish New Year, and concluding with *Yom Kippur* ten days later, a day of atonement and fasting. I plan to attend Congregation Sha'ar Zahav, whose rabbi, Yoel Kahn, was such a support and presence during Barbara's dying. I particularly need connection with other Jews, with the continuity of ceremony and ritual, with the sounds of ancient words and songs that have reassured and comforted me in the past. I schedule the necessary surgery for the day after *Yom Kippur* and begin to enter my own sacred time.

Much of it is spent re-creating our apartment to suit my aesthetic, my taste, my needs. It is time, at this start of the Jewish New Year, at this pause between diagnosis and surgery. During those ten days, I attend synagogue and sift through rooms filled with papers and books. I find the files containing early drafts of Barbara's dissertation written nearly twenty years before. I empty, clean, reread everything. Lying in bed, in the midst of what had been, in another lifetime, the guest room, I sort through crumpled envelopes of old pictures and arrange them in six new scrapbooks. Later I pack four large cartons filled with Barbara's assortment of books. Experimental novels, travel books, research methodology with her scrawled notes in the margins; books she had used to prepare classes a decade before. The desk stands where our bed had once been, the most generative spot of the apartment. Where we loved and where Barbara died. Above it I have hung a framed notecard from Barbara, sent years before, in which she wished me great creativity and energy, and the ability to craft loving and wise words. Now her face smiles down at me as I try to honor her wish.

During these weeks I chisel a home from the cluttered excess we had created together. I pare down, simplify, create plain, austere rooms. A home that will contain me within it. Reflect and cradle me as I prepare for surgery.

October 4

After breaking the *Yom Kippur* fast, I entered the hospital and in two days emerged with a scar across my throat, marking the spot where my thyroid had been. Unlike Barbara, I have no staples holding my incision together, no gauzy bandage absorbing its fluids. Tidy, small, contained, quite unlike her extravagant scar.

My newly decorated apartment, under Alison's expert supervision, fills with women, food, laughter, relief. My body appears to know just how much sleep and how much energy it can expend at every moment. Somewhat akin to passion, I remember, where the mind has no useful information for the body. The body bodies.

Now I begin to believe in a good prognosis with no change in my life span. I reread a letter written during those first days to my friend Riek, "This experience feels like one in which I have been lifted up by giant hands and shaken. A gentle but firm remonstration. What was it that needed to be said, I wonder?"

November 6

Today I had my quarterly gynecological examination, more frequent than most because in 1956, as a young, pregnant wife, I was given DES to "hold" the baby. Now I'm closely watched; a Pap test several times a year. The doctor called and asked me to return because of a "very common, minor abnormality."

After further examination, she suggests taking a biopsy "to be sure" everything is as it should be. "Of course," I murmur, with equal reassurance. "Whatever needs to be done." I have confidence in this woman. In her training, her skills, her empathy, and in her politics. I settle back for the cramping she prepares me for but which doesn't occur. "There's been so little traffic there," I weakly tease. She grins, relieved I am taking this procedure so well. I return her grin, my face masking the terror that spreads through me.

I want to get out of here. One floor below this examining room is Kathy Grant's office. There had been so much bad news each time I'd entered there. Now I am afraid that this same building will house my bad news, my diagnosis, my chemotherapy infusions, my blood counts, my tears. I need to get out of here—will say anything I need to get out of here.

Returning home, I sink gratefully into the welcoming sofa, pour a glass of wine, and try to get back to normal. Dinner, correspondence, phone calls to return. A life in process. My life.

"What is the worst that can happen?" I had asked her as I was dressing.

"Perhaps a cone biopsy, just to clean up the errant cells. It's a one-day, outpatient procedure. We do it all the time."

I remember when they inserted a catheter into Barbara's chest after her veins collapsed and they couldn't stick her for blood or chemo infusions anymore. That, too, was to be a one-day, outpatient procedure. She was full of pain as I sat beside her, blindly flipping the pages of a six-month-old *Good Housekeeping* magazine.

Then suddenly I am ashamed of the comparison. Dysplasia isn't life and death, I remind myself. Neither was my thyroid cancer. Only scary, intrusive, disruptive.

I miss Barbara so now. The emptiness of the house surrounds me. The silence. The tidiness. I long for the smell of onions cooking, the sound of big band music, the sight of socks wadded in a corner behind the chair. The apartment I have created, one that was to be uncluttered, serene, and peaceful, now feels sterile and empty and I begin to weep.

November 19

For the next several weeks, I have been instructed to stop taking artifical thyroid supplement. This abrupt withdrawal is required to force my body to become hypothyroid, so that a scan can be taken to assure there is no further spread of disease. "Prepare," one doctor told me "for low energy."

"No," said another, "more like depression, emotional paralysis. There may be an inability to make decisions or even to remember why it's important to do so."

I listened to them both but did not believe their cautionary words would apply to me. Just as cancer had not—up to then—applied to me. There was so much unreality about this advice, this disease process, that I nodded solemnly and ignored their words.

The first week I was exhausted by late afternoon, sleeping deeply each night only to awaken feeling heavy and sluggish. Unpleasant, I thought, but manageable. Akin, perhaps, to a cold that relievedly doesn't blossom into a flu. Then the depressive symptoms began, and I spent hours ruminating about my life, my choices, my failures. Mostly, my failures. It's my *body*—not my psyche—I reminded myself. But I grew frightened, and early each morning I left the house to walk for several hours just to tire myself. I thought about Barbara's mother, who still flings herself out onto the Boardwalk on Coney Island every day to walk until she can sleep. I remembered thinking what a good strategy she's found to handle her depression. Never understanding the desperate urgency to keep moving. Of feeling on fire and needing to move—like bubbles dancing on a hot stove. This morning I understand. Finally I returned home exhausted, heart pumping, calmer.

December 7

Now I am unable to leave the house, to drive a car, to take a walk. "You have no reflexes," the doctor warns. He's right. Even colors are too stimulating. Music, the concentration required to read, the focus necessary for speech have all evaporated, along with my thyroid.

Pam again takes me, now scarcely able to move around at all, to the hospital, where I lie on a gurney after drinking radioactive isotopes, as my body is scanned to be sure there is no "activity" of errant cancer cells in my body. To be sure the surgery "got it all." I lie passively on the table for several hours, first once, then again a few days later, while they redo the procedure. Pam waits for me, as I waited for Barbara. I am too listless to feel frightened: I just feel the table move, dimly hear voices, blurry, just beyond my vision, and wait for them to tell me I can go home. It's like moving through fog in an unfamiliar landscape. Later the doctor calls to say everything is fine. Like my Pap test was fine. They will "watch me closely." Another Pap test in a few months. Another body scan in six months.

I am filled with relief and guilt. I will not die.

December 11

During most of my life with Barbara, Bruce and Cameron lived upstairs, close friends and roommates, filled with health, energy, passion. We had barbecues in the garden, took in each other's mail when we were away, and lived in a companionable closeness. But Barbara died, then just a year later Cameron's young, wiry body yielded to AIDS, and now Bruce has begun to fail. This is his third bout of pneumocystis and he has returned from the hospital, weakened and spent.

We had talked often of going to Sha'ar Zahav together during the past years but had never managed to find the time. Now I prepare to celebrate the first night of Chanukah and the ritual lighting of the *menorah* with him, as he is too weak to leave the house.

I carry the *menorah* upstairs as he lies, puppet-like, attached to strings of wire and tubing, his lover, Scott, beside him. I light the first candle, repeating the traditional prayer, and then we talk of the meaning of the lights and the ways it illuminates our days, our acts, our world. We speak of struggle, injustice, faith, insistence on a world of freedom, and of God in each of us.

December 12

I have just checked on Bruce, lying upstairs watching gymnasts on television. In the dimly lit room, he watches young men and women pumped up with health and fitness, in control of their bodies.

Crossing to his bed, I place my hands on his face, lean over, and press my lips to his young, soft ones. I am an old star, he whispers, and he a comet. "Thank you for anchoring me to the galaxy," he continues, his voice scarcely audible. "Thank you for being in my life."

"I love you," I say finally. All there is left to say.

December 26

So many symmetries. Bruce's death at home so like Barbara's. A calm readiness. A loving partner. I watched him, blond hair tufting through his baseball cap, as he lay weighing only 120 pounds, with Barbara's lap desk across his bony hips, completing his good-bye cards. I still see her in my mind's eye, sprawled, bloated, across our bed, writing to each person in a quavery handwriting about living in the service of Tikkun Olam, where each act mends, restores, and transforms the world.

January 1991

Now it is the start of another year, one in which my cancer, after necessary scans and testing, appears to be completely eliminated; my Pap test is unremarkable. My thyroid replacement medication has begun to work and I feel more energetic. Bruce died as he wished, at home, in bed, with Scotty beside him. He, too, wanted us to scatter his ashes in the garden.

I am left with the ordinary urgencies of daily life. But now it is a dailiness embedded in the sacred. In the unexpected richness of being human. I am left, finally, with gratitude.

February 14

THE THIRD ANNIVERSARY OF BARBARA'S DEATH. This morning, while taking a walk, I passed a convalescent home, its windows filled with very old men and women peering out at the street through cloudy panes of glass. I caught the eye of an old woman, smiled, and waved at her as her face exploded with pleasure, delighted to be seen. She lifted her frail arm to return my wave and unexpectedly then, I began to weep. For Cameron. For Bruce. For Barbara. For myself. For all the women and the men who have died. For the losses that burden my heart and the determination that allows me to endure. With love.

Appendices

Cancer in Two Voices
Video Project

The companion video and 16mm film based on this book, also called
Cancer in Two Voices, is available from:

Women Make Movies, Inc.
462 Broadway, 5th Floor,
New York, NY 10013
Phone: 212-925-0606
Fax orders: 212-925-2052

The video, by Lucy Massie Phenix, includes extensive interviews
with Sandy and Barbara. It is appropriate for educational and activist
screenings, and is available for rental. Contributions of time, distribution expertise, and post-production funding are always welcome.

Sociologists for Women in Society
Barbara Rosenblum Fellowship
for the Study of Women and Cancer

The Barbara Rosenblum Fellowship for the Study of Women and Cancer was established with a bequest from Barbara Rosenblum, a member of Sociologists for Women in Society since 1972. The purpose of the fellowship is to encourage doctoral research in sociology, anthropology, psychology, and related fields on women's experience of breast cancer and the prevention of breast cancer. The yearly award goes to a woman scholar "with a feminist orientation who is sensitive to studying breast cancer and its impact on women of color as well as white women, on lesbians as well as heterosexuals, and women from diverse social classes and cultural backgrounds." The fellowship committee wants to support research that has practical applications and can be presented to lay audiences as well as to social scientists.

Before her death, Barbara wrote that "since 1972, SWS has been the major organization in my life to which I have devoted my caring and political affiliations . . . Because SWS has been so important to me, I want to set up a research fund to encourage the study of women's experience of breast cancer."

For donations or inquiries contact:
Mary French
062 Rike Hall
Wright State University
Dayton, OH 45435
e-mail: mcfrench@desire.wright.edu

Other Titles Available From Spinsters Ink

All the Muscle You Need, Diana McRae	$8.95
Amazon Story Bones, Ellen Frye	$10.95
As You Desire, Madeline Moore	$9.95
Being Someone, Ann MacLeod	$9.95
Cancer in Two Voices, 2nd Ed., Butler & Rosenblum	$12.95
Child of Her People, Anne Cameron	$10.95
Common Murder, Val McDermid	$9.95
Considering Parenthood, Cheri Pies	$12.95
Desert Years, Cynthia Rich	$7.95
Elise, Claire Kensington	$7.95
Fat Girl Dances with Rocks, Susan Stinson	$10.95
Final Rest, Mary Morell	$9.95
Final Session, Mary Morell	$9.95
Give Me Your Good Ear, 2nd Ed., Maureen Brady	$9.95
Goodness, Martha Roth	$10.95
The Hangdog Hustle, Elizabeth Pincus	$9.95
High and Outside, Linnea A. Due	$8.95
The Journey, Anne Cameron	$9.95
The Lesbian Erotic Dance, JoAnn Loulan	$12.95
Lesbian Passion, JoAnn Loulan	$12.95
Lesbian Sex, JoAnn Loulan	$12.95
Lesbians at Midlife, ed. by Sang, Warshow & Smith	$12.95
The Lessons, Melanie McAllester	$9.95
Life Savings, Linnea Due	$10.95
Look Me in the Eye, 2nd Ed., Macdonald & Rich	$8.95
Love and Memory, Amy Oleson	$9.95
Martha Moody, Susan Stinson	$10.95
Modern Daughters and the Outlaw West, Melissa Kwasny	$9.95
Mother Journeys: Feminists Write About Mothering, Sheldon, Reddy, Roth	$15.95
No Matter What, Mary Saracino	$9.95
The Other Side of Silence, Joan M. Drury	$9.95
Ransacking the Closet, Yvonne Zipter	$9.95
Roberts' Rules of Lesbian Living, Shelly Roberts	$5.95
Silent Words, Joan M. Drury	$10.95
The Solitary Twist, Elizabeth Pincus	$9.95
Thirteen Steps, Bonita L. Swan	$8.95
Trees Call for What They Need, Melissa Kwasny	$9.95
The Two-Bit Tango, Elizabeth Pincus	$9.95
Vital Ties, Karen Kringle	$10.95
Well-Heeled Murders, Cherry Hartman	$10.95
Why Can't Sharon Kowalski Come Home? Thompson & Andrzejewski	$10.95

Spinsters titles are available at your local booksellers or by mail order through Spinsters Ink. A free catalog is available upon request. Please include $2.00 for the first title ordered and 50¢ for every title thereafter. Visa and Mastercard accepted.

Spinsters Ink
32 E. First St., #330
Duluth, MN 55802-2002

218-727-3222 (phone)   spinsters@aol.com   (fax) 218-727-3119

Spinsters Ink was founded in 1978 to produce vital books for diverse women's communities. In 1986 we merged with Aunt Lute Books to become Spinsters/Aunt Lute. In 1990, the Aunt Lute Foundation became an independent nonprofit publishing program. In 1992, Spinsters moved to Minnesota.

Spinsters Ink publishes novels and nonfiction that deal with significant issues in women's lives from a feminist perspective: books that not only name these crucial issues, but—more important—encourage change and growth. We are committed to publishing works by women writing from the periphery: fat women, Jewish women, lesbians, old women, poor women, rural women, women examining classism, women of color, women with disabilities, women who are writing books that help make the best in our lives more possible.

photo by Sandra Butler

BARBARA ROSENBLUM, a creative sociologist, taught at Stanford University and Vermont College, and was widely published during her life in anthologies, journals and magazines ranging from the *American Journal of Sociology* to the *San Francisco Chronicle* to *Sinister Wisdom.* Her book, *Photographers at Work* (Holmes and Meier, 1978), was an early entry in the emerging field of the sociology of aesthetics. After a passionate career as a writer and teacher, Barbara died of breast cancer at age 44.

photo by Lynda Koolish

SANDRA BUTLER'S ground-breaking book, *Conspiracy of Silence: The Trauma of Incest* has become a classic source and reference guide to the complex issues of incest. *Cancer in Two Voices*, written in collaboration with Barbara Rosenblum, was the winner of the Lambda Literary Award for Lesbian Non-Fiction in 1992. It is a personal document of living and dying, designed to make the private experience of terminal illness public, and thereby, political.

Butler's trainings and seminars are attended by therapists, trainers, organizers, and others interested in the relationship of personal growth to social change activism. In her work, participants embed the personal, the private, the individual dimensions of their lives in the public, the political, and the structural realities of women's lives.

In addition to her work with those in the field of child sexual assault and the politics of women's health, she is the Co-Director of the Institute for Feminist Training. In this capacity, she specializes in training, supervision, and program consultation with individuals working in all forms of feminist psychological theory and practice, political organizing, and cross-cultural work.